Reprinted in 2010
First published in 2007 by New Holland Publishers (UK) Ltd
London • Cape Town • Sydney • Auckland
Garfield House, 86–88 Edgware Road, London W2 2EA, United Kingdom
www.newhollandpublishers.com
80 McKenzie Street, Cape Town 8001, South Africa
Unit 1, 66 Gibbes Street, Chatswood, NSW 2067, Australia
218 Lake Road, Northcote, Auckland
Copyright © 2007 text AG&G Books
Copyright © 2007 illustrations and photographs New Holland Publishers (UK) Ltd
Copyright © 2007 New Holland Publishers (UK) Ltd
ISBN 978 1 84537 482 2
10 9 8 7

Editorial Direction: Rosemary Wilkinson Edit⋯ ⋯ Konopelski Production: Hazel Kirkman
Designed and created for New Holland b⋯ ⋯s Copyright © 2004 "Specialist" AG&G Books
Design: Glyn Bridgewater Illustrations: D⋯ ⋯idgewater, Coral Mula and Ann Winterbotham
Editor: Alison Copland Photographs: ⋯ ⋯nt ⋯⋯⋯: John Fleming
Reproduction by Pica Digital Pte L⋯ ⋯⋯⋯
Printed and bound in Malaysia by T⋯⋯⋯ ⋯ (M) Sdn Bhd.

The information in this book is ⋯ue an⋯ ⋯⋯⋯ ⋯⋯ ⋯ be⋯⋯ ⋯⋯ ⋯⋯dge. All recommendations
are made without guarantee on the part ⋯ the authors and the publishers. The authors and publishers
disclaim any liability for damages or injury resulting from the use of this information.

ALLOTMENT

Specialist

**The essential guide to
preparing, planting, improving
and maintaining an allotment**

A. & G. Bridgewater

Contents

Author's foreword **2**

Author's foreword

When I first saw my allotment, I was amazed. It was another world. The whole place was throbbing with people happily digging, planting and just enjoying themselves. There were children playing in overgrown corners, old folk quietly working away at their plot, people sitting and resting outside their sheds, old men brewing tea on little gas stoves, young couples with barrow-loads of produce, a single mothers' group complete with a crèche, a group from the local school, and so on.

My family and I soon came to realize that allotments are more than just vegetable plots – they are a way of life. The more we became involved, the more exciting it became. We made friends, we learnt new ways of gardening, we became interested in organic gardening, we had exercise, we cut our food bill, and we ate till we burst; it was great.

As if all that was not enough, we soon came to learn that allotments are a haven for wildlife. We all moan and groan about slugs, snails, wood pigeons and other 'pests', but there is something very special about seeing foxes, badgers, rabbits, mice, slow worms, toads and lizards all red in tooth and claw.

Do not worry if you are a beginner; this book will show you how to get the best out of your allotment. You are invited to roll up your sleeves, take up the challenge and get started. Good luck!

Measurements

Both metric and imperial measurements are given in this book – for example, 1.8 m (6 ft).

SEASONS

This book is aimed at readers in the UK, so both months and seasons are used – early spring, mid-spring, early April, late October and so on. Although advice is given on the best time to sow, plant, tend and gather, because of regional variations you will have to be flexible and ready to modify dates to suit the mini climates that may exist in your area. In some northerly areas, spring may begin several weeks later than in more southern regions.

Allotments and community gardens

Allotments are more popular than ever. In fact, in inner cities there are now long waiting lists. If you have preconceived notions and think of allotments as being the last refuge for flat caps, old men and bicycles, think again. My neighbouring holder does wear a large tweed cap – but it looks fine with her green wellies, designer swimwear, sunglasses and suncream – and holders are just as likely to arrive in an expensive car as on a bicycle.

Are allotments dying out?

The perfect allotment – a variety of fruits and vegetables growing strongly, plenty of colourful flowers, and lots of sunshine and silence.

A SHORT HISTORY

Although the history of allotments goes way back to a time when commoners were 'allotted' land, allotments really came into prominence in 1914 with the first world war, and later in 1939 with the second world war when people were encouraged to 'dig for victory'. Since the self-sufficiency movement in the 1960s and the organic movement in the 1990s, allotments have become places where busy people grow the best of the best, work out to good effect, and generally mingle with like-minded people. As for size, the average allotment measures approximately 10 rods, or 253 square metres (302 square yards) – and is described by various Acts of Parliament as being 'a plot big enough to feed a family of four'.

COMMUNITY GARDENS

Some allotment-holders do in fact turn their patch into a sort of community garden complete with a vegetable plot, ponds, patios, children's playing areas, and a few animals. If it encourages people to get involved with growing and eating good food, then it has to be good.

IS AN ALLOTMENT RIGHT FOR ME?

If you want to meet people, enjoy the best organic food, keep fit, commune with nature, experience the 'good life' and generally 'get back to the way it was', then you are going to enjoy having an allotment.

ADVANTAGES AND DISADVANTAGES OF HAVING AN ALLOTMENT

Advantages

✔ You can grow most of your own food

✔ Gives you a chance to eat fresh food

✔ Cost of an allotment is minimal – about £20 a year – with reductions for pensioners

✔ Gives you plenty of exercise – very therapeutic

✔ Good way of meeting a cross-section of people with differing personalities and outlooks

✔ Good for families with kids – educational and good fun

✔ Many allotments allow small animals such as chickens, rabbits and goats

✔ Can be run more like a smallholding than a vegetable patch

Disadvantages

✘ Can be hard work

✘ Distance between allotment and home can be annoying

Choosing an allotment

Apart from all the important factors that have to do with security of tenure – important because it takes several years of cropping to repay the initial costs and hard labour involved with setting up – a good allotment plot must have a fair aspect, a good depth of reasonable soil, just the right amount of shade and shelter, and a source of water. You must get it right, because any start-up mistakes may cause failure even when other conditions are favourable.

A carefully chosen allotment can be turned into a haven – a place for you to work, rest and sometimes just dream the day away. Ideally, the plot should be open to the sun and there should be protection from wind on the north and northeast boundaries.

IS LOCATION IMPORTANT?

Location is everything. Look for a piece of land in a generally level area that has a gentle slope facing towards the southeast or the southwest, so that either morning or evening sun sweeps across the plot. The plot should be unshaded by trees, but protected on the north and northeast sides by hedges, walls, trees or fences.

DO I HAVE A CHOICE?

Contact your local authority for information on the various allotments in and around your area. There are sometimes long waiting lists, so you might find that your choice is fairly limited and you just have to take what you are offered.

CAN I HAVE MORE THAN ONE PLOT?

In areas where there is a waiting list you can only have one plot, even though some longstanding tenants within that allotment might have more than one. In areas where there is plenty of land you can usually have as many plots as you like.

ALLOTMENT RULES

Allotments are normally leased for a period of one year. The tenancy lease agreement will set out all the rules and regulations. For example, you cannot be a nuisance, sublet, run a business, surround your plot with barbed wire, build structures larger than a specified size, keep animals without controls and so on.

Look for these ...

- A small allotment that is within easy walking distance of your home.
- An allotment with links with local community groups and schools.
- A gently sloping plot with a southeast or southwest aspect and an edge-of-allotment boundary to the northeast.
- A plot with protection on the north and east sides.
- A plot that has been well worked by an experienced allotment-holder.
- A plot with a good depth of soil: a 60 cm (2 ft) deep hole should show, from top to bottom, 5–7.5 cm (2–3 in) of turf, about 30 cm (1 ft) of rich brown topsoil, and a clay, gravel or sand subsoil.
- Good free drainage.
- A plot that is surrounded by healthy-looking, productive plots.
- A plot with a water trough or a standpipe within easy reach.

Avoid these ...

- Brownsite land where there is evidence of concrete and rubble, such as the site of an old factory.
- An allotment that it situated on low-lying boggy ground.
- A plot with trees to the south side.
- A plot that shows signs of spraying with pesticides and weedkillers.
- An overgrown plot that has been used as a general dumping ground – a plot piled high with weeds, old plastic bags, tangled wire and so on.
- An allotment that shows evidence of being vandalized, such as broken fences, broken huts and graffiti.

THE IDEAL ALLOTMENT PLOT

Of course the ideal allotment plot is something of an impossible dream – a sort of rosy picture of how it could be – but it is something to aim for nonetheless. When you eventually get your plot, walk around it at various times of day and see how it sits with the sun. Decide how you can build a small greenhouse, a shed and various fences and shelters without annoying any of your neighbours. Spend some time talking to neighbouring plot-holders.

Shed
A good shed with lots of glass on the southwest side

Cold frames
Used for hardening off seedlings

Permanent beds
Beds set aside for crops such as herbs, artichokes, asparagus and rhubarb

Seed beds
One or more of these will be needed

Orientation
The plot should slope gently to the southeast or southwest

Secondary paths
Use these to divide the large beds so that you can rotate crops within them

Water-butt
Essential to collect the precious rainwater run-off from the shed

Patio
A hard area for resting, eating, drinking and socializing

Storage
Bins, boxes and butts used for storing items such as canes, plastic sheet and netting

Compost
Bins or boxes used for composting

Manure
A heap in the process of rotting down

Fruit cage
A permanent structure for soft fruit

Windbreak
Include a low windbreak on the northeast side

Cloches
Frames covered with plastic sheet, fleece or netting

Gentle incline
The ground needs to have just enough of a slope to shed water

Fruit trees
Plant low, slow-growing or trained fruit trees on the east side of the plot

Crop rotation
Divide the total plot into three distinct main areas or beds so that you can more easily rotate crops

Water supply
Ideally, this should be within walking distance

Boundary path
A good path defines the outer limits of the plot

Drainage
A drainage trench around the boundary is a good place to put stones and rubble

Sheds, tools and water-butts

What sort of shed do I need?

On an allotment you can, within the rules set down in various pieces of legislation, build just about any shed that takes your fancy. Your allotment will have its own specific regulations, and of course the shed does need to be functional and safe, but the rest is up to you. I know of a shed that was made from the back end of a sailing boat, and another that appears to be made entirely from a mishmash of old oak-framed windows.

This new plot is just beginning to take shape, with some healthy-looking crops, a small shed and a handy water-butt.

SHED OPTIONS

Small, apex-roofed shed with a side window

Medium-sized, pent-roofed shed with a front window

Large shed with an integral greenhouse section

Low-cost option with double doors and no window

Shed made from 'found' components such as old windows and salvaged wood

DIY building tradition

Because the history of allotments involved giving, or allotting, poor people some land so that they could grow sufficient food to feed a family of four throughout the year, a tradition developed whereby modern-day allotment-holders build their sheds from salvaged materials. The good thing about this is that, where it was once a make-do-and-mend necessity, it is now an eco-aware boast to say that the shed has been built entirely from old packing cases or other recycled materials.

DO I NEED A SHED?

Of course, much will depend on just how far you live away from your allotment, but you do need a shed to hang your tools, prepare your seed-trays, and store all the buckets, bags and other items involved with tending your plot. A shed is also the perfect place to sit and have a cup of tea, and to shelter from the rain.

INSIDE THE SHED

The ideal shed has plenty of hooks and nails on which to hang your tools, the biggest bench that space allows, one or more good-sized windows, an old chair, a place to store such things as buckets, bags and a wheelbarrow, and maybe room to store a mower. The shed does not need to be particularly large or lavish, but it does need to be secure and watertight.

A tool section complete with tool rack, wooden trough with oiled sand, and locker.

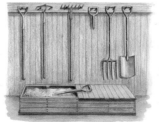

A well-designed worktable is the perfect place to while away a rainy day.

SHED REGULATIONS

Regulations vary from one allotment to another, so it is a good idea to start by talking to your allotment committee. My particular committee allows me to build a structure that is no larger than 1.5 m (5 ft) wide, 2.1 m (7 ft) long and 2.1 m (7 ft) high at its highest point. It can be made from new or salvaged materials as long as it is painted black or dark brown. The shed must be sited at least 60 cm (2 ft) away from the nearest path, and its general position must be approved by neighbouring plot-holders.

A friend's allotment committee allows just about any structure on one of their plots, as long as it is safe and the owner has made it vandalproof.

TOOLS AND MATERIALS

- **Spade** You need a spade for digging – one that suits your height and strength. It is much better to go for a lightweight spade than one that is too heavy.
- **Fork** Some people have two forks – one with slender prongs for general digging and one with flat prongs or tangs for digging up root crops.
- **Rake** An indispensable tool used for breaking up the surface of newly dug soil, and for preparing seed beds.
- **Hoe** There are two types: the Dutch hoe with its double-edged blade that is used with a push-and-pull action for cutting out weeds; and the swan-necked draw hoe that is used for preparing seed beds and earthing up.
- **Dibber** The dibber or dibble is a pointed tool used for making holes – for planting potatoes, bean seeds and such. You can make one from a broken wooden fork or spade handle.
- **Trowel and hand fork** Tools used for digging small holes, for loosening up the soil prior to planting, and for lifting small plants.
- **Secateurs and loppers** Useful scissor-like tools for cutting sticks and twigs.
- **Pegs and string** These are invaluable for such tasks as marking out lines of vegetables, and trimming the edges of grass paths.
- **Plastic netting** Useful for keeping birds off crops, and for supporting taller plants.
- **Canes** Lengths of bamboo used for supporting plants, holding netting and countless other tasks.
- **Plastic pots** You need a supply of different-sized flower pots for potting and repotting plants.
- **Seed trays** Used for raising plants from seed, and for growing seedlings until they are large enough to be put into flower pots or planted outside in the soil.
- **Cell trays** Like seed-trays, but divided into little cells or pockets. Designed so that seedlings can be lifted complete with their root systems.
- **Watering-can** You need at least one large watering-can.
- **Wheelbarrow** A wheelbarrow is useful for all the various earth-shifting tasks.
- **Bucket** You need at least one bucket, for such tasks as carrying water and taking produce home.
- **Water-butts** Most plot-holders tend to have one or more plastic water-butts or old baths to collect the rainwater that flows off their shed. Certainly, they sometimes look a bit messy, but they are a good way of saving water, and of saving all the effort involved with walking backwards and forwards from the standpipe or water trough to the plot.

SOME BASIC EQUIPMENT

A selection of the tools and materials you are likely to need is illustrated below. Knee pads may be a useful addition to this list, and if you have an area of lawn you will also need a mower and lawn-edge trimmers.

Spade Fork Rake Hoe Dibber Trowel Hand fork Secateurs Loppers Pegs and string Scissors Gloves Plastic netting Canes Seed-tray Cell tray Fibre pot Fibre cell tray Bucket Watering-can Wheelbarrow Plastic pots

A source of water in the form of a butt is vital, especially if the plot is a long way from a standpipe

Vandalism

In my experience, vandalism is on the increase. Always be on your guard, although there is little you can do about mindless vandalism such as graffiti and smashed-down plants, other than to see that the whole allotment is fenced and looks cared-for.

Theft

Always lock up your tools when you leave the plot. As for what you can do to prevent someone taking a liking to your crops, the best advice is to leave your plot looking tidy and cared-for, so that they think you are close by.

Preparing the soil

Are there any shortcuts?

As my grandfather used to say, the only way to prepare the soil properly is to roll up your sleeves and just do it. You can use a flame-thrower to burn the weeds, a rotovator to stir the soil, and various other 'labour-saving' options, but the only real way to get the job done is to dig it by hand. If you take a comfortable spade and dig a couple of spade-widths every day (perhaps a few more if the sun is on your back), the job will be done in no time.

HOW TO DIG CORRECTLY

Mark out a clod with three vertical cuts of the spade. Slip the blade down behind the clod, slide your hand down towards the base of the handle, and lift and turn the clod over on itself. Rest a moment and then repeat the procedure.

ROTOVATING BY MACHINE

In my experience, rotovators are more trouble than they are worth. They are expensive, always breaking down, hard work on the back, noisy, they conflict with the eco-friendly philosophy of the allotment, and, worst of all, they chop the weeds up. As if all that is not damning enough, the 'mush' of weeds is buried just a few centimetres (inches) below the surface, ready to sprout again.

Left: A nicely prepared plot. Note the grass paths that provide access to the beds, complete with clean-cut edges.

SINGLE DIGGING

Divide the plot down the middle of its length. Take out one 'spit' or 'trench' – the depth and width of the spade – from the first half and lay the soil down on one side. Add manure or compost to the trench bottom. Remove the thin layer of weeds from the second trench and lay it upside-down in the first trench. Take out the soil from the second trench to the depth of one spit and lay it over the weeds in the first trench. Rerun the procedure down to the end of the plot. Move to the second half and continue. When you get to the end of the second half, put the contents of the first spit that you dug into the last trench.

Pros – The close contact with the soil tells you a lot about its quality.
Cons – The activity is rather time-consuming.

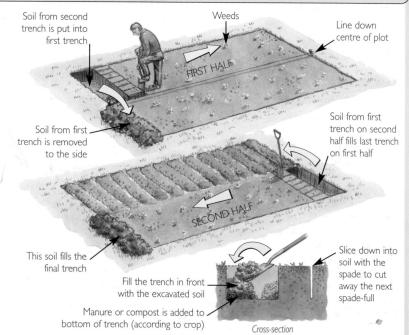

Soil from second trench is put into first trench

Weeds

Line down centre of plot

FIRST HALF

Soil from first trench is removed to the side

Soil from first trench on second half fills last trench on first half

SECOND HALF

This soil fills the final trench

Fill the trench in front with the excavated soil

Manure or compost is added to bottom of trench (according to crop)

Slice down into soil with the spade to cut away the next spade-full

Cross-section

DOUBLE DIGGING

Divide the plot down the middle of its length. Take out two 'spits' – so as to finish up with a trench about 60 cm (2 ft) wide – and lay the soil down on one side. Add manure or compost to the trench bottom and turn it over to the full depth of a fork. Skim the turf about 5 cm (2 in) deep from the next two spits and lay it upside-down in the first trench. Take out the soil from the next two spits and lay it over the turf so as to fill up the first trench. Repeat the procedure down to the end of the plot. Move to the second half and continue. When you get to the end of the second half, put the contents of the first two spits that you dug into the last trench.

Pros – Although the soil is broken up to two spits deep, the subsoil remains undisturbed.

Cons – It is very hard work.

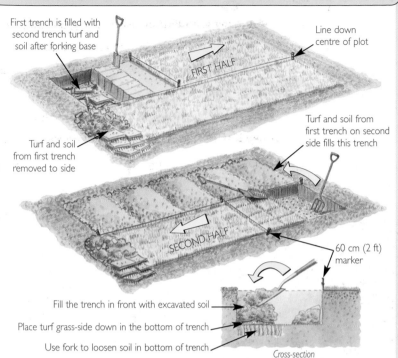

First trench is filled with second trench turf and soil after forking base

Line down centre of plot

FIRST HALF

Turf and soil from first trench removed to side

Turf and soil from first trench on second side fills this trench

SECOND HALF

60 cm (2 ft) marker

Fill the trench in front with excavated soil

Place turf grass-side down in the bottom of trench

Use fork to loosen soil in bottom of trench

Cross-section

TRENCHING

Divide the plot down the middle of its length. Take out a trench about 45 cm (18 in) wide and two 'spits' deep and lay the soil on one side. Dig out the top spit from the next 45 cm (18 in) wide trench and lay it down on one side. Dig out the bottom spit from the second trench and put it in the first trench. Now dig out the top spit from the third trench and fill up the first trench. Remove deep-rooted weeds as you go. Continue the sequence for the length of the plot. Move to the second half and continue the process.

Pros – The ground is broken up to a depth of three spits and enriched with vegetation.

Cons – It involves a lot of time and effort.

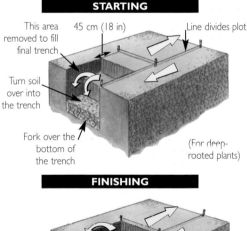

STARTING

This area removed to fill final trench

45 cm (18 in)

Line divides plot

Turn soil over into the trench

Fork over the bottom of the trench

(For deep-rooted plants)

FINISHING

Turn soil over to make up the level in the first trench (removing any weeds)

PREPARING A TRENCH

Return the soil to the trench

Fork the manure into the soil in the bottom of the trench

Fertile soil

To prepare a single trench for planting, say, beans or marrows, dig out a 45 cm (18 in) wide trench one spit deep, and put the soil on one side. Fork well-rotted manure and/or compost into the bottom of the trench, to the full depth of the fork. Return the topsoil to the trench.

Compost

What can I compost?

It is best to use vegetable matter of a soft texture, manure, and vegetable peelings and scraps from the kitchen. Leaves, grass and hedge clippings, kitchen peelings, small amounts of newspaper, old tea bags, dead flowers and crop residues, manure from farmyard animals such as horses, cattle and goats, and bedding from vegetarian pets such as rabbits and guinea pigs are all good. On no account use dog and cat faeces or cooked meat.

GARDEN COMPOST AND GROWING COMPOST

There can be some confusion regarding the term 'compost'. On the one hand there is the compost that we use as a soil improver – all the stuff that we put on the compost heap – and on the other there are the specially formulated compost mixes that we use for growing seeds and plants. One of the basic tenets of having an allotment involves recycling, so many growers also make their own growing media from their composted waste.

JOHN INNES COMPOSTS

'John Innes' composts are not actually a commercial product, but rather formulas that were developed at the John Innes Institute in the early years of the twentieth century. The different types use various mixes of loam, peat, sand and fertilizer.

Do add to compost
• Farmyard and stable manure • Manures and bedding from vegetarian pets • Fruit and vegetable peelings and scraps • Soft plant waste from the allotment • Paper and card • Flower, grass and weed clippings • Natural fabrics such as cotton and wool

Do not add to compost
• Glass • Metal cans • Unused medicines • Dog or cat faeces • Dead animals • Any sort of cooked or uncooked meat • Plastics • Paint, oils or solvents • Synthetic fabrics such as nylon • Disposable nappies • Rampant weeds

MAKING COMPOST

Well-made compost is a good substitute for farmyard manure. Take your weeds, vegetable peelings and all the rest and spread it in a 15 cm (6 in) layer. Water the layer and sprinkle it with sulphate of ammonia and superphosphate of lime, or a proprietary decay accelerator. Continue in this way, adding another layer, a sprinkling of accelerator, and so on, until the heap is complete. The heap can be built all at once in a few hours, or over weeks or even months.

COMPOST CONTAINERS

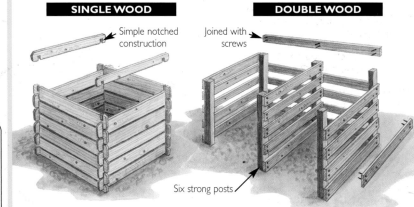

SINGLE WOOD

Simple notched construction

DOUBLE WOOD

Joined with screws

Six strong posts

COMMERCIAL COMPOST CONTAINERS

Commercial bins or containers made of plastic are not as easy to use as, say, a large wooden-box type, but they are a good option if you have no choice other than to build a little-by-little, as-you-go heap, using small amounts of kitchen scraps. Plastic bins are generally a bit of an eyesore, and they veer away slightly from the make-do-and-mend philosophy, but they do get the job done. Make sure that you get one made from recycled materials.

WORM FARMS

Worm farms are a fun option in that the worms will turn your waste into top-quality compost – perfect for making into a growing medium – much more efficiently than a traditional compost bin. You can buy a ready-made worm farm complete with worms, or you can make a worm bin from a plastic dustbin and buy in the worms. My children were very happy to help me with my worm farm.

Manure and fertilizers

Manure is defined as a bulky material of an organic and natural origin, a material that supplies a lot of humus, such as a mix of cow or horse excreta and straw. A fertilizer is a more concentrated source of plant food with little or no humus, that might be organic or inorganic. So, for example, a nitrogen fertilizer can be obtained from organic materials such as blood and bones, or from inorganic materials such as mineral nitrate and nitro chalk.

What is the difference?

MANURE – NOT JUST SMELLY!

Manures can be smelly, but they are essential sources of humus, which is vital for the maintenance of soil structure. The more humus you get into the soil, the better its fertility. Humus holds moisture, supplies food to plants, and generally prevents the soil from becoming impoverished. If you have the choice between cow, horse, pig or poultry manure, horse manure is the one to go for. Stable manure is easy to handle, it is high in nitrogen, and it is more fibrous and richer than, say, cow manure. Rabbit manure is very good, but it is usually only available in small quantities.

DO I NEED FERTILIZERS?

The natural world – forests and jungles – is self-sustaining; there is no waste and no need for fertilizers. The cycle of life goes round and round – animals and plants grow, feed on each other, die, and compost down, enriching the soil naturally. If you work at it, you can maintain soil fertility, and control pests and diseases, simply by recycling, making composts and using manures. Fertilizers are a poor short-cut option.

THE ACID-ALKALINE BALANCE

Soils never stay still in their acid-alkaline balance. Apart from the fact that some soils are inherently more acid than others – clay is more acid than sand, for example – all soils become more acid under cultivation. You can test the balance, and you can hold the acidity levels by spreading lime, but it is always best to grow plants that are known to thrive in your particular soil.

TYPES OF MANURE

Stable manure: Fibrous – about 0.6 per cent nitrogen. Good for heavy soils and for making hotbeds. Easy to handle, low in cost, and readily available from farms and stables.

Cow manure: Wet – about 0.4 per cent nitrogen. Good for light sandy soils. Difficult to handle unless it is mixed with lots of absorbent material such as straw.

Poultry manure: Smelly and rich – about 1.8 per cent nitrogen. Good for ground that is resting. Can be a bit messy to handle – very smelly and wet.

Rabbit manure: A rich warm smell – high in nitrogen. Very good if you can get enough of it. My supply comes as a mix of manure and sawdust, and is very convenient and easy to handle.

Seaweed: A rich smell – about 0.5 per cent nitrogen. Pleasant to handle, rots readily and can be obtained free.

Types of fertilizer

Chemical fertilizers: Some chemical fertilizers, such as various nitrates, have long been considered by traditionalists as being somehow 'damaging'. The thinking is that, while these artificial nutrients are fine in the short term, they do long-term damage to the structure of the soil. It is therefore best to use organic fertilizers.

Bone meal: Good organic fertilizer – swift-acting. Apply in late winter or early spring. Good for root growth.

Guano: Traditional fertilizer, now difficult to obtain. Helps to build up humus levels.

Fish meal: Good general fertilizer, and eco-friendly if the meal is a by-product.

Hoof and horn meal: Slow-release source of nitrogen, which promotes good leaf and root growth.

Wood ash: The quality varies. Eco-friendly if it is a by-product of a managed forestry activity. High in potash.

HOW TO USE MANURE

Manure can be spread when the ground is frozen and dug in when the ground has thawed, with the ground being left until the following growing season, or it can be spread as a thick mulch. If you do spread fresh manure as mulch, be careful that it does not come into direct contact with salad crops. Wear gloves and wash your hands afterwards.

HOW TO USE FERTILIZERS

Fertilizers can be spread on the soil as a dry powder or pelleted dressing, or mixed with water and poured on. Be wary when you are spreading dusty organic fertilizers, such as bone meal, that you do not inhale the dust. Always wear gloves, and wash your hands afterwards. Also be aware that some organic growers object to fertilizers.

Plant and plot rotation

Different crops use up different nutrients from the soil. If you keep planting brassicas in the same plot, for example, the soil will become depleted of nitrogen and the plants will become sick. Therefore you should not grow the same kind of crops, one after another, on the same kind of soil. Crop rotation helps preserve the balance between the plant foods in the soil, and helps keep a check on various pests and diseases.

A GOOD LAYOUT

When you are dividing the land up into four plots – for permanent crops, brassicas, legumes and salad plants, and root vegetables – try to set it out so that the individual plots can be planted with the rows running in a north–south direction. If you look at the layout shown here, you will see that the permanent plot is on the north side, so that, while the structures give some protection from cold winds, they do not cast long shadows. You should keep a plan of the cropping – perhaps in the form of a diary – so that you can refer to past years when you are making plans for the years to come.

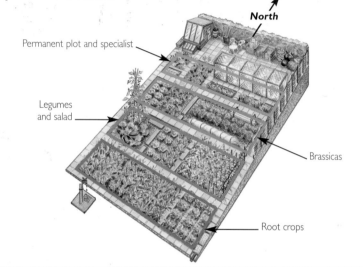

North

Permanent plot and specialist

Legumes and salad

Brassicas

Root crops

THREE-YEAR ROTATION PLAN

Although the longer the rotation the better, on an allotment it is best to divide the ground up into four plots, with one plot being put aside for permanent crops and specialist vegetables, and then manage the other three plots on a three-year rotation. This scheme can be taken one step further by rotating the crops within the individual plots. So, for example, even though the root vegetables will be grown in plot 1 the first year, then in plot 2, then plot 3, and back to plot 1 in the fourth year, when you come around to planting them in plot 1 you can plant them in a different position, so that, say, carrots follow potatoes, swedes follow beetroots, and so on.

Permanent plot (not rotated)

The following crops are defined as 'permanent' in the sense that they can remain in or near the same bed for a number of years.

- Asparagus – can be left in the same bed for 10–20 years.
- Globe artichoke – reaches its peak in the third or fourth year.
- Bay – a hardy evergreen shrub; likes a well-

drained, moisture-retentive soil in a sunny position.

- Borage – a hardy annual.
- Chervil – a hardy biennial that is usually grown as an annual.
- Chives – a hardy, low growing, clump-forming perennial.
- Dill – a hardy annual.
- Fennel – a hardy herbaceous perennial.

- Mint – a hardy herbaceous perennial.
- Parsley – a hardy biennial.
- Rhubarb – can be left in the same bed indefinitely.
- Rosemary – an evergreen shrub.
- Sage – a hardy evergreen shrub.
- Thyme – a hardy dwarf evergreen shrub.

Specialist vegetables (not rotated)

The following crops are defined as 'specialist' for no other reason than that they can be grown in the permanent plot. • Tomatoes • Marrows and courgettes • Aubergines • Capsicums

THREE-YEAR ROTATION PLAN (CONTINUED)

Brassicas (rotated)

Brassicas and plants that enjoy the same soil conditions

• Broccoli

• Brussels sprouts

• Cabbage

• Cauliflower

• Kale

• Kohl rabi

• Radish

Legumes and salad (rotated)

• Runner beans

• French beans

• Broad beans

• Celeriac

• Endives

• Lettuces

• Onions and shallots

• Peas

• Beet leaf

Root vegetables (rotated)

Root vegetables and plants that enjoy the same conditions

• Beetroot

• Carrots

• Chicory

• Parsnips

• Potatoes

• Swedes

• Turnips

• Salsify

• Leeks

• Spinach

• Sweetcorn

• Celery

YEAR 1

ROOT VEGETABLES	LEGUMES AND SALAD	BRASSICAS
POTATOES	RUNNER BEANS	BROCCOLI
	LETTUCE	BRUSSELS SPROUTS
	PEAS	
SPINACH / PARSNIP / SWEET CORN	LETTUCE	CABBAGE
	PEAS	
	LETTUCE	
CARROT		RADISH
BEETROOT	BROAD BEANS	
SWEDE		KALE
CELERY	BEET LEAF	
TURNIP	ONION	CAULIFLOWER
LEEK	ENDIVE	
SALSIFY		RADISH
PARSNIP	FRENCH BEAN	
CHICORY	CELERIAC	KOHL RABI

YEAR 2

LEGUMES AND SALAD	BRASSICAS	ROOT VEGETABLES
RUNNER BEANS	BROCCOLI	POTATOES
LETTUCE	BRUSSELS SPROUTS	
PEAS		
LETTUCE		SPINACH / PARSNIP / SWEET CORN
PEAS	CABBAGE	
LETTUCE		CARROT
BROAD BEANS	RADISH	BEETROOT
		SWEDE
BEET LEAF	KALE	CELERY
ONION		TURNIP
ENDIVE	CAULIFLOWER	LEEK
		SALSIFY
FRENCH BEAN	RADISH	PARSNIP
CELERIAC	KOHL RABI	CHICORY

YEAR 3

BRASSICAS	ROOT VEGETABLES	LEGUMES AND SALAD
BROCCOLI	POTATOES	RUNNER BEANS
BRUSSELS SPROUTS		LETTUCE
		PEAS
CABBAGE	SPINACH / PARSNIP / SWEET CORN	LETTUCE
		PEAS
RADISH	CARROT	LETTUCE
	BEETROOT	BROAD BEANS
KALE	SWEDE	
	CELERY	BEET LEAF
	TURNIP	
CAULIFLOWER	LEEK	ONION
	SALSIFY	ENDIVE
RADISH	PARSNIP	FRENCH BEAN
KOHL RABI	CHICORY	CELERIAC

Catch crops and intercropping

What is the difference?

Catch cropping and intercropping are both used to maximize the growing potential of the plot. Catch crops are rapidly growing vegetables that can be grown in a vacant plot, while intercropping is a system in which fast-growing vegetables are grown alongside slow-growing ones. For example, radishes can be grown alongside celery, and lettuces grown alongside beans. The disadvantage of both systems is that the closeness of the plants encourages pests and diseases.

A catch-crop mix of tomatoes, beetroot and carrots is not only productive but also wonderfully attractive.

These relatively fast-maturing lettuces are being grown as an intercrop alongside sweetcorn (top) and carrots (right).

IS THIS AS COMPLICATED AS IT SOUNDS?

In the sense that fast-growing crops can be planted in vacant ground or planted between slow-growing plants, both systems are relatively easy and straightforward. The complexity comes when the planting is so close that the plants have to compete for light and air. That said, some plants seem to benefit by growing between other plants. If you are short of space, you have the choice of intensively catch cropping and intercropping, or growing the crops in beds so that the plants are more or less touching each other.

Companion planting

Companion or beneficial plants are those that appear to benefit by being grown together. For example, French marigolds seem to discourage whitefly when they are grown alongside cabbages, and onions seem to offer some protection against carrot fly. Try it and see if it works…

THE BENEFITS

The benefits are that the plot is used to its full potential. You are not left with empty ground, and you do not have to prepare the ground other than to fork or rake it over. The two systems allow you to take advantage of what you see happening on the ground. If you see that a certain patch is empty, or there is space between slow-growing crops, or a line of crops has failed, then all you do is plant fast-growing varieties that can take advantage of the situation. The system allows you to be spontaneous and to cash in on what would otherwise be a waste of space.

Lettuces and radishes: In late March, sow a packet of mixed-variety lettuces in rows 10–13 cm (4–5 in) apart. Sow lines of mixed-variety radishes between the rows. Pick the radishes and lettuces when they are ready.

Lettuces and peas: Sow an early pea in mid-March in rows 38 cm–1.2 m (15–48 in) apart, depending on the variety. In early April, sow successive lines of lettuces between the rows. Harvest both crops when ready.

Lettuces, carrots and cauliflowers: Sow four lines of lettuces 30 cm (1 ft) apart in early April. In mid-April, sow a line of carrots between the middle two rows of lettuces. In late April, sow cauliflowers between alternate lettuces in the outer rows.

MORE INTERCROPPING IDEAS

The following examples show a range of intercropping options.

Example 1

February
Plant two rows of cabbage lettuces 30 cm (1 ft) apart with 30 cm (1 ft) between the rows.

March
Plant cauliflowers between every second lettuce. Also sow carrots between the two rows.

May
Clear the lettuces and set pot-grown dwarf beans between each cauliflower.

June
Harvest the cauliflowers, and put the beans and carrots in.

July
Dig two trenches and plant celery. Plant spinach or lettuces between the celery. Follow the celery on with parsnips, carrots and beet.

Example 2

March
Plant second early potatoes.

August
Lift the potatoes and plant both large and small varieties of cabbages 30 cm (1 ft) apart in rows 60 cm (2 ft) apart.

October
Plant cabbage lettuces 20 cm (8 in) apart in a row between the rows of cabbages.

December
Harvest the small cabbages.

February
Clear the last of the small cabbages and plant broad beans in their place.

April
Harvest the last of the lettuces and sow a row of runner beans to fill the space.

January
Having picked the runner beans and dug the plot, plant shallots.

June
Having harvested the shallots, dig in manure and plant with celery 30 cm (1 ft) apart in rows 38 cm (15 in) apart. Sow radishes between the rows.

Example 3

October
Plant cos lettuces in rows 30 cm (1 ft) apart.

February–March
Sow dwarf peas between alternate rows of lettuces.

June–July
Pick peas and plant broccoli 45 cm (18 in) apart in rows 60 cm (2 ft) apart. Sow cabbage lettuces between the rows.

May
Clear the ground and dig in some manure. Plant pot-grown cucumbers.

August
Plant cauliflowers between the cucumbers.

Weed control

What is a weed?

A weed is just a plant that is growing in the 'wrong' place. You might spend a lot of time, money and effort getting poppies and daisies to grow in a meadow – good, beautiful, they are just where you want them – but if the self-same poppies and daisies decide to take over your allotment they are weeds. A weed might be anything from a biennial or a shrub to a tree or even a vegetable. Hand-weeding is the easiest and most selective option for controlling them.

COMMON WEEDS AND HOW TO REMOVE THEM

The following list of weeds includes the ones you are most likely to find on your allotment.

BINDWEED
A deep-rooted perennial. The root must be dug out. Any small piece of root will grow into a new plant. Cover freshly dug ground with plastic sheeting and keep hoeing and forking the ground.

CHICKWEED
An annual, easy to get rid of, provided you do not let it seed. Hoe off young seedlings and pull up established plants. The shallow roots can be removed by forking over the ground.

COUCH GRASS
A creeping perennial. Hoe and fork over, and remove by hand – try to take out all the roots. Repeat this procedure at regular intervals.

CREEPING BUTTERCUP
A persistent perennial. Hand-weeding is most effective, with either a trowel or a grubber. Keep the ground forked over and remove the young plants as soon as they appear.

DANDELION
A persistent perennial. Hand-weed with a grubber or slender trowel. Cut down before seeding. If vacant neighbouring plots are overrun with dandelions, cover them over with plastic sheeting.

GROUNDSEL
An annual that is relatively easy to get rid of, providing you do not let it seed. Hoe it off in the young stage, or pull it up by hand. Keep the ground forked over and remove the weed as soon as it reappears.

MARESTAIL
A creeping persistent perennial that can only be removed by deep digging. Little bits of root will grow into new plants. A pernicious weed that is very difficult to eradicate. Keep forking the ground over and removing young plants.

NETTLE
A creeping persistent perennial. Grub up the roots and burn them. Keep forking the ground over and remove the creeping roots.

WHEN TO WEED

You need to be weeding all the time. Fork over the ground in spring to remove roots, cut them down as soon as they flower, and cover the ground with plastic sheeting if the ground is empty. Hand-weeding and forking simply to remove weeds is a thankless task. The best approach is to remove the weeds along the way – as part of a more interesting task. For example, when you are involved in the pleasuresome business of lifting your potatoes, or digging trenches to plant marrows, you can also be on the lookout for weeds. It does not feel so much like hard work when weeding is a side activity to the main event.

DIGGING, HOEING AND MANUAL REMOVAL

In reality, most of the deep-rooted persistent weeds need to be removed by hand – digging, hoeing or pulling. It is an ongoing activity. If you watch an experienced allotment-holder at work – say, digging – he will turn a clod over, remove a few weeds and roots, stand up to stretch his back, dig out another clod, remove another root or two, and so on. It will be much the same when he comes to hoeing around plants. He will be stirring the soil with his hoe, inspecting plants, grubbing up the odd deep-rooted weed and generally on the lookout for problems.

MORE WEED PREVENTION AND REMOVAL METHODS

Mulching

SPENT MANURE

↗ Cover the ground with a layer of spent manure, which stifles the weeds and enriches the soil.

LIVING MULCH

↗ Cultivate a low-growing plant such as Trefoil, which smothers the weeds and can be dug in at the end of the season.

HOE MULCH

↗ Stirring the top centimetre (inch) or so of the soil with a hoe creates a loose layer, which will keep down the weeds and hold in the moisture.

Woven plastic

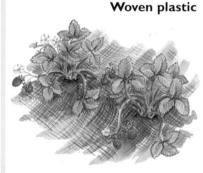

↙ Cover the ground with a long-lasting woven-plastic membrane, which keeps the weeds down and allows water into the soil.

Wood chip

↙ Cover the ground with a thick layer of wood chips – it smothers the weeds, allows for easy weeding, and can be dug in at the end of the season.

Burning off

Using a flame-thrower to burn the weeds off from a new allotment does at least allow a beginner to get started – and some people like the drama of it all – but it is expensive and messy, and worst of all unnecessary.
It is much easier to cover the ground with old carpet or plastic sheeting and then dig the ground little by little.

Chemical weedkillers

When I was a child in the 1950s, gardeners and farmers were using chemicals prolifically. If they did not like a certain weed or beetle, then a good spraying did the trick. Now look where we are – just as many weeds, poor soil and problems with our wildlife. Once you know that there is no such thing as a 'safe' weedkiller, it is easy to see that the only approach is simply not to use chemical weedkillers.

Protecting plants

Why is this necessary?

Plants need protection from a variety of things, as described below. Not so long ago, we had greenhouses, glass cloches, glass bell jars, canvas screens and mats, wood and glass cold frames, straw baskets, sticks and strings, and that was about it. Now we have all the old methods, plus plastic polytunnels, plastic cloches, plastic sheeting, fleece in all manner of types and thicknesses, recycled plastic bottles, and so on. Plant protection has never been easier.

Polytunnels and plastic-covered greenhouses are fast becoming a good, low-cost, practical option for protecting susceptible plants in bulk.

WHAT DO PLANTS NEED PROTECTION FROM?

Apart from the elements – wind, frost, sun and rain – your plants need to be protected from insects that are looking for a place to lay eggs, as well as hungry birds, mice, squirrels, and so on. The disadvantage is that the plants will need regular watering, the warm atmosphere will encourage some pests, and of course if you keep off all the birds then you will not benefit from the birds eating the pests.

TYPES OF PROTECTION

Improvised methods

➔ There is a healthy make-do-and-mend tradition on allotments that has to do with making cloches and screens from salvaged windows. Simple A-frame cloches make good no-cost cloches – perfect for protecting young seedlings.

Two old windows secured with pegs and rope

Cloches

↘ ➔ Glass cloches are good, but plastic tunnel cloches are better. A few bent sticks or wires covered with plastic make very good, easy-to-move, long-lasting, low-cost mini-tunnels.

Clear plastic sheeting supported on bent canes

Shop-bought cloche system using clear plastic corrugated sheeting

Recycling

➔ Clear plastic drinks bottles make very good, no-cost mini-cloches that are perfect for growing seedlings. Safer and easier to use than glass.

Recycled clear plastic water containers

Greenhouses

➔ Traditional greenhouses are a good option in a garden, but perhaps not such a good idea on an allotment. Ask around to see if stone-throwing children plague your allotment.

A traditional brick, wood and glass greenhouse

WINDBREAKS

As well as causing physical damage – blowing structures over and breaking plants – winds can lower the overall soil temperature. You could build low-level windbreaks to help alleviate this problem.

Hedges and fences A good hedge is the ideal, but a well-built fence can be very useful. If time and space allow, you could make a woven willow screen or maybe even create a living willow screen by cutting thin willow wands and pushing them into the ground.

Clear plastic sheeting tied to poles

Plastic screens A plastic screen might not be very pretty, but it will go a long way to protecting your plants from the worst of the wind. Use stout posts and salvaged plastic sheets to build temporary screens.

Low-level 'baffles' These can be built to protect specific plants – use posts and salvaged corrugated plastic sheeting, arranged so that the plants are sheltered in the lee of the structure.

Corrugated plastic sheeting tied to stakes

PEST DETERRENTS

Slugs and snails The best way of dealing with slugs and snails is to leave lots of upturned pots and trays lying about, so that they are lured in, and then gather them by hand.

Butterflies and beetles My grandfather used to drape old net curtains over his cabbages to keep off the dreaded white butterflies – and it worked a treat. Now you can do much the same thing with the various grades of horticultural fleece. It is a great idea – it lets in air, light and water, but keeps out butterflies, carrot flies and all manner of bugs and beetles.

Birds Sticks and strings are good, but better still are some of the open mesh fabrics. The best method is to protect the plants when they are tender – to keep off pigeons and the like – and then remove the nets when the plants have toughened up.

Rabbits The best way of keeping out rabbits is to ring your plot around with a knee-high fence made from rabbit mesh, with 30 cm (1 ft) or so buried below ground level.

USING A CONE

Based on the traditional basket and matt cones used by the Victorians, the modern DIY cone is no more than a cane wigwam, stuffed loosely with straw and wrapped around with plastic sheeting. It provides really good protection for vulnerable plants.

MORE PROTECTION IDEAS

My grandfather used to say something like 'one line for the birds and one line for us'. In many ways, the best defence is no defence. All you do is let the whole of nature in, and let the various creatures sort it out among themselves. You will find that you will be able to achieve a natural balance, with plenty of food all round.

DISEASE PREVENTION

To a great extent, you can keep the level of disease down by running a 'clean ship'. If you keep the soil in good order, choose healthy plants that like the conditions, use disease- and pest-resistant varieties, group plants so that they benefit from each other, rotate the crops, remove blackfly and aphids as soon as they appear, and generally keep the plot clean and tidy, you will, at the very least, reduce the problems.

The best option is to encourage the number of animals that feed on the pests. For example, you could build bird boxes to encourage insect-eating birds such as blue tits, and you could have a small pond to bring in frogs, toads, lizards, slow worms and all the other predators that feed on garden pests. If you do feel the need to use a spray, then go for one of the soft soapy options. They will not do much more than wash the pests off the plants, but they will not hurt the plants or the animals that are looking to feed on the pests you have just washed off.

Year-round calendar

The following year-round calendar will not answer all the questions – because your soil conditions and weather patterns are specific to your area, and perhaps you will not want to plant all the vegetables on offer – but it will give you a basic framework and timetable to work to.

JANUARY Inspect your tools; sort out things such as stakes, pots, plastic sheets and fleece. Set seed potatoes to sprout, order seeds, plan the plots for sowing. **Soil** – Turn over vacant soil, double dig if weather permits, spread manure, and order seeds. **Sowing and planting** – Plant broad beans in a warm spot. Sow onions, leeks and radishes in a frame or hotbed. **Harvesting** – Pick sprouts, winter cabbages, last of the carrots, celery, chicory, and anything else that is ready.

FEBRUARY Clean up paths, and generally make sure that all your gear is in good order. Cover frames over at night. Look at your plot and see if you can get ahead with more digging. **Soil** – Use the fork, hoe and rake to prepare seed beds – look for a nice warm corner and make sure there is a good even tilth. Remove weeds; put rubbish in the compost heap. **Sowing and planting** – Plant artichokes and shallots. Sow early peas and maybe another row or two of broad beans. Sow carrots, lettuces and radishes under glass on a hotbed. Raise seedlings in warm frames, things such as leeks, cucumbers, onions and tomatoes. **Harvesting** – Pick Brussels sprouts, winter cabbages, last of the carrots, celery, chicory, and anything else that is ready.

MARCH Weed paths, mend fences, keep digging up weeds. Look at your plot and see if you want to change this around, especially the arrangement of the permanent plot. **Soil** – Break down and rake the surface of double-dug plots. Keep stirring with the hoe and generally be on the lookout for weeds – especially deep-rooted perennials. **Sowing and planting** – Sow hardy seeds out of doors – lettuces, parsnips. Sow things such as spinach, broccoli, leeks, onions, peas, celery, tomatoes and marrows under glass, either directly in the bed or in trays. **Harvesting** – Pick Brussels sprouts, cabbage, cauliflower.

APRIL Check for slugs and snails. Watch out for problems on fruit trees and bushes. Thin out seedlings as necessary. Reduce the number of sprouts on seed potatoes. Cover cold frames at night. **Soil** – Keep working the ground with the hoe along the rows of seedlings. Draw the soil up on potatoes. **Sowing and planting** – You can now sow just about anything in the open. Plant maincrop potatoes. By the end of the month plant onions, radishes, maincrop carrots, beet, salsify and scorzonera, endives, kohl rabi, more lettuces, peas and spinach. Plant out any seedlings that you have hardened off, such as Brussels sprouts. Sow runner beans, marrows and courgettes under glass. **Harvesting** – Pick beet leaf, broccoli.

MAY Be ready to protect tender seedlings. Watch out for blackfly on beans. Set twigs among the peas. Put mulch around fruit trees and bushes. Reduce the number of runners on the strawberries. Water seedlings. Keep on hoeing and weeding. **Soil** – Prepare more seed beds. Hoe and rake regularly. Earth up potatoes. Mulch between rows of more advanced vegetables. **Sowing and planting** – Plant out hardy seedlings from the frames. Sow tender vegetables in the open. Sow beans in the open – French, runners and broad. Sow more peas, endives, radishes and summer spinach. Plant out Brussels sprouts, broccoli, cucumbers. **Harvesting** – Pick beet leaf, broccoli, early beetroot, early carrots, cucumbers under glass, endives and numerous other vegetables.

JUNE Bring in fresh manure. Keep everything well watered. Spread mulches around turnips. Put nets over fruit. Remove weak canes from the raspberries. Clean out cold frames and keep on hoeing and weeding. Stake up runner beans and peas. **Soil** – Keep hoeing. Dig up potatoes. Fork over vacant seed beds. **Sowing and planting** – Plant out seedlings from the nursery beds. Sow succession crops such as endives, lettuces and radishes. **Harvesting** – Pick anything that takes your fancy.

JULY Stake plants that look hot and weary. Gather soft fruits as and when ready. Cut mint and herbs ready for drying. Topdress with manure. Look at the tomatoes and pinch out and feed as necessary. Lift and dry potatoes. Keep hoeing between crops. Water and weed. Make sure that the greenhouse and frames are open to the air. **Soil** – Weed and hoe. Weed after lifting potatoes. Earth up maincrop potatoes. **Sowing and planting** – Plant out celery, cabbage, Brussels sprouts and broccoli. **Harvesting** – Keep picking, eating and storing.

AUGUST Order seeds for autumn sowing. Keep storing vegetables for the winter – bottling, drying and freezing. Bend over the necks of onions. Dry herbs. Pinch out the tops of tomatoes. Clear and dig the ground. Protect fruit crops from the birds. Plant out new strawberry beds. Keep forking, hoeing and weeding. **Soil** – Weed and hoe. Dig and fork over empty potato plots. **Sowing and planting** – Make more sowings of endives, radishes, spinach, onions and anything else that fits the season. Sow lettuce and salad crops under glass. Sow cabbages for spring planting. **Harvesting** – Keep picking, eating and storing. Dry more herbs; gather beans, tomatoes and fruit as and when they are ready.

SEPTEMBER Protect crops from frosts if necessary. Lift and store roots. Earth up celery and leeks. Watch out for and destroy caterpillars. Prune raspberries. Water, weed and hoe as necessary. Blanch endives. **Soil** – Weed and hoe. Dig, fork and rake the moment you have cleared the crops. Earth up plants as needed. **Sowing and planting** – Plant out spring cabbages. Look at your seed packets and sow if possible. **Harvesting** – Lift potatoes and onions. Gather runner beans. Lift and store roots. Gather and store tree fruits as they ripen. Keep picking and eating other crops as and when ready.

OCTOBER Watch out for frost and protect as needed. Start digging vacant plots. Continue hoeing and weeding. Clear the ground and add to the compost heap. Clean up paths and edges. Thin onions. **Soil** – Weed and hoe. Dig and fork over plots as they become vacant. **Sowing and planting** – Plant rhubarb and fruit trees. Sow peas in a protected cold frame. Sow salad crops under glass. Plant out seedlings. Sow early peas in warm areas. **Harvesting** – Gather the rest of the tomatoes. Lift and pick celeriac and carrots.

NOVEMBER Watch out for frost and protect as needed. Clean up leaves and debris. Dig vacant plots. Continue hoeing and weeding as necessary. Remove bean and pea sticks and poles. **Soil** – Weed and hoe. Dig and fork over plots as they become vacant. **Sowing and planting** – Sow broad beans in a sheltered spot. **Harvesting** – Lift and store root crops. Cut, lift and eat other crops as needed.

DECEMBER Watch out for frosts and protect as needed. Clean the tools and the shed. **Soil** – Weed and hoe. Dig and fork over plots as they become vacant. Fork the soil over so as to expose pests. Check that stored vegetables are in good order. **Sowing and planting** – If the weather is very mild, you could plant broad beans. Draw earth up around the peas. Sow salad crops under glass and protect as needed. **Harvesting** – Pick the last of the beet leaf. Pick Brussels sprouts, winter cabbages, last of the carrots, celery, chicory and anything else that is ready.

Quick-reference sowing calendar

The following table gives the sowing times, the distance between seeds and the distance between rows for a wide variety of vegetables. It is useful as a rough guide and reminder but does not replace the instructions provided with your seeds.

QUICK-REFERENCE SOWING CALENDAR

CROP	SOWING TIME	DISTANCE BETWEEN SEEDS	DISTANCE BETWEEN ROWS
Beans, broad	May–February	13–20 cm (5–8 in)	45–60 cm (18–24 in)
Beans, French	April–July	5–7.5 cm (2–3 in)	30–60 cm (1–2 ft)
Beans, runner	May–June	13–15 cm (5–6 in)	1.5–2.4 m (5–8 ft)
Beetroot	March–July	7.5–15 cm (3–6 in)	30 60 cm (1–2 ft)
Broccoli	April–May	45–90 cm (18–36 in)	60–90 cm (2–3 ft)
Brussels sprouts	March–April	45–90 cm (18–36 in)	45–90 cm (18–36 in)
Cabbages (spring)	July–August	30–60 cm (1–2 ft)	30–60 cm (1–2 ft)
Cabbages (summer)	February–May	30–60 cm (1–2 ft)	30–60 cm (1–2 ft)
Cabbages (winter)	April–May	30–60 cm (1–2 ft)	30–60 cm (1–2 ft)
Capsicums	February–March	45 cm (18 in)	45 cm (18 in)
Carrots	March–July	5–7.5 cm (2–3 in)	15–30 cm (6–12 in)
Cauliflowers	March–May	45–60 cm (18–24 in)	60–90 cm (2–3 ft)
Celeriac	March–April	30 cm (1 ft)	25–60 cm (10–24 in)
Celery	April	15–30 cm (6–12 in)	0.9–1.2 m (3 4 ft)
Courgettes	April–May	60 cm (2 ft)	1.2–1.5 m (4–5 ft)
Cucumbers (outdoor)	May–June	60 cm (2 ft)	60–90 cm (2–3 ft)
Cucumbers (indoor)	February–April	60 cm (2 ft)	60–90 cm (2–3 ft)
Kale	April–June	45–60 cm (18–24 in)	60–90 cm (2–3 ft)
Kohl rabi	March–April	13–15 cm (5–6 in)	25–30 cm (10–12 in)
Leeks	February–March	15–30 cm (6–12 in)	30–60 cm (1–2 ft)
Lettuces	March–September	25–30 cm (10–12 in)	30–60 cm (1–2 ft)
Marrows	April–May	60 cm (2 ft)	1.2–1.5 m (4–5 ft)
Onions	March–August	5–15 cm (2–6 in)	23–30 cm (9–12 in)
Parsnips	February–April	13–15 cm (5–6 in)	30–45 cm (12–18 in)
Peas	March–July	13–15 cm (5–6 in)	60 cm–1.5 m (2–5 ft)
Potatoes	March–May	30–45 cm (12–18 in)	45–90 cm (18–36 in)
Radishes	January–September	2.5–5 cm (1–2 in)	10–23 cm (4–9 in)
Salsify	April–May	13–15 cm (5–6 in)	25 30 cm (10–12 in)
Scorzonera	April–May	13–15 cm (5–6 in)	25–30 cm (10–12 in)
Shallots	March	23 cm (9 in)	23–30 cm (9–12 in)
Spinach (perpetual)	April–July	15–20 cm (6–8 in)	30–45 cm (12–18 in)
Spinach (summer)	February–August	23–30 cm (9–12 in)	30–38 cm (12–15 in)
Spinach (winter)	July–September	15 cm (6 in)	30–38 cm (12–15 in)
Swedes	April–July	15–23 cm (6–9 in)	38 cm (15 in)
Tomatoes (under cover)	February–March	60 cm (2 ft)	90 cm (3 ft)
Tomatoes (outdoor)	March–May	45 cm (18 in)	90 cm (3 ft)
Turnips	April–August	15–23 cm (6–9 in)	30–38 cm (12–15 in)

Preparing a seed bed

What is a seed bed?

Apart from seeds that are germinated in pots and trays under glass to give them an early start, most seeds are sown directly out in the allotment in carefully prepared beds. They might be sown in drills and then thinned out and left in place – as with, say, carrots or radishes – or they might be sown and then transplanted as seedlings to a final growing position. Either way, the original prepared piece of ground is described as a 'seed bed'.

A well-prepared seed bed with a mini-wall to deter slugs and snails.

Seed-bed tools

You will need all of the following tools and materials:

- Fork to prepare the top few centimetres (inches) of soil.

- Swan-necked hoe to break up clods of earth and to prepare drills.

- Rake to create a fine tilth.

- Large-mesh sieve for stony ground.

- String line and marking pegs. You could use cheap natural fibre string and leave it in place so as to show where not to put your feet.

- Dibber and trowel.

- Plank – either plain or marked off in centimetres or inches.

- Marking stick set out in centimetres or inches.

- Nets to protect the seeds from birds.

- Selection of cloches and tunnels to keep the seeds warm.

- Selection of low-level windbreaks to protect vulnerable plants.

- Bucket to collect all the rubbish that you rake off.

- Two watering-cans, one with a fine rose attachment.

HOW TO PREPARE A SEED BED

Sometime in early spring, go out into the allotment and test the soil. If it sticks to your boots, it is not ready, but if it is dry on the surface and nice and moist and friable just below the surface, then it is ready. Use a hoe and rake to break and rake the top 7.5–15 cm (3–6 in) of the surface to a smooth finish. Continue working this way and that, backwards and forwards, all the while breaking up the lumps, raking the surface, removing large stones and bits of stick, until the soil looks and feels level.

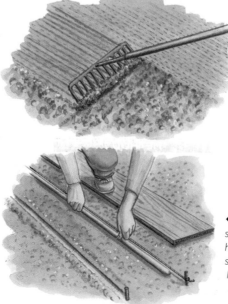

Levelling

← Use both sides of the rake to work the soil to a good finish – the back of the rake to drag high spots into hollows, and the tines or teeth of the rake to break the soil into smaller and smaller pieces.

Making a drill for fine seeds

← Set the hoe or rake down on the prepared soil, so that the head is uppermost, and press hard down on the handle so as to make a shallow, half-round impression that is about 18 mm (¾ in) wide and 6 mm (¼ in) deep.

HOW TO PREPARE A SEED BED (CONTINUED)

Making a drill for medium seeds

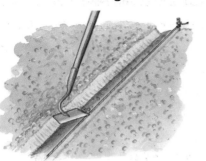

↙ *Mark the position with pegs and string. Take a swan-necked hoe, hold it at a slight angle and drag it along to one side of the line to make a shallow V-section trench. Make the V-section shallower or deeper to suit the size of your seeds.*

For large seeds or seedlings

↙ *Mark out the position with pegs and string. Take a dibber and a distance-apart measuring stick, and set off along the line dibbing holes. Choose the stick and make the holes deep enough to suit your seeds.*

TROUBLESHOOTING

Sticky soil: If the soil is sticking to your hands, it is probably still too wet.

Wet weather: Ideally, choose a day on which the weather is damp and overcast.

Stones: You do need to move large stones – meaning ones that are going to get in the way of the seeds – but apart from that you can leave stones since they aid drainage.

Tree roots: If there are a lot of tree roots, your plot is probably going to be overshadowed. Chop small roots out with a sharp spade.

Protection: The best option is to cover the seeds up the moment that they are in the ground. Use sticks and string, netting, fleece – anything to keep off pigeons, mice and other pests.

Watering: Use a watering-can fitted with a fine rose for small seeds, and a can with a spout to 'puddle in' seedlings.

RAISED BEDS

What are raised beds?

Raised beds are no more than little enclosures that allow you to raise the soil up above the level of the underlying ground.

Advantages of raised beds

Raising and containing the soil is a good option on at least five counts – you do not have to stoop so low, you do not need to step on the soil, the plants are to some extent protected from pests, the soil in the bed can be modified to suit the plants, and the sides of the containment make it easier to keep out the weeds.

METHOD 1

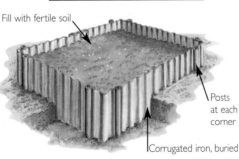

Fill with fertile soil

Posts at each corner

Corrugated iron, buried

↙ *Use corrugated plastic or metal sheeting to create a bed. Dig the sheeting deep into the soil so that the wavy end is uppermost. Support it with posts banged into the ground. This is a good option for keeping invasive plants such as mint in, and creeping weeds out. You could cover the sharp edge of the corrugated sheeting with strips of wood or plastic.*

METHOD 2

Fill with fertile soil

Lengths of wood nailed or bolted together

↙ *Use large section wood to build a heavy frame that sits on the ground. You could use short lengths of railway sleeper, or perhaps lengths of salvaged wood. Building sites are a good source for offcuts of ceiling and floor joists.*

Seed-sowing and planting

Do I need 'green fingers'?

Good gardening, thriving allotments, successful planting and so on involve inspiration, trial-and-error research, lots of reading and old-fashioned hard work. When you see so-called green-fingered gardeners in action – in books, on the television or in the flesh – it is clear that they are, above all, enthusiastic and hardworking. So, when sowing seeds and planting seedlings, if you put in the required effort and generally do your best, you cannot help but be a winner.

When the seedlings are large enough to handle, prick them out into individual pots, taking care not to damage them.

These onion sets have been carefully laid out in rows, at the correct spacings, on well-prepared ground, before being pushed directly into the soil.

Growing from seed versus buying seedlings

The best option is to grow your own plants from seed. It is cheaper, you know precisely what varieties you are getting, you can have all the fun of watching the seeds grow, and, best of all, you avoid the risk of bringing in diseases and pests.

ABOUT SEEDS

Seeds vary in size from those that are big enough to handle individually – as with peas and beans – to those that are so small that they are sown by the pinch.

ABOUT SEEDLINGS

Seeds grow to become seedlings. Seeds that have been sown directly in the ground are thinned out at the seedling stage. Seeds of root crops such as carrots must be sown directly into the ground because they cannot be transplanted. Seeds that have been germinated in boxes are pricked out into pots, or into the ground so that they can be grown to a bigger size.

ABOUT BULBS

Crops such as onion sets and shallots are unusual in that they are grown from individual bulbs that are pushed directly into the soil.

ABOUT TUBERS

Potatoes are reproduced by underground tubers, which grow and develop to produce clusters of tubers.

SEEDLINGS IN TRAYS

1 *Cover the drainage holes with bits of broken crock, fill the tray with moist growing compost, and use a wooden board to press it down firmly.*

2 *Use a folded piece of paper and the tapping action of your fingertips to gently distribute the seeds.*

3 *Use a sieve to cover the seeds with a sprinkling of compost so that the layer suits the type of seed.*

4 *Repeat the pressing procedure and then water the whole tray by lowering it into a bowl of water.*

SEEDS IN POCKETS

1 Overfill the pocketed tray with a suitable growing compost and then level it off with a length of wood.

2 Use a firm tapping action in order to consolidate and level the compost within the pockets.

3 Sow one or more seeds in each pocket; the number depends on the predicted germination rate. Thin multiple sowings to the best individual seedlings.

4 Use a watering-can fitted with a fine rose to water the whole tray so that the compost is moist rather than wet.

Compost pots

Compost pots are a very good option for relatively delicate plants such as tomatoes, in that the pot becomes part of the rootball. The plant, pot and all, is planted on.

Other methods for seeds

You can sow seeds in anything from shop-bought trays and pockets to salvaged yogurt pots, old egg boxes, and bits cut from plastic drinks bottles. Cardboard egg boxes make very good fibre seed pockets.

PROPAGATORS

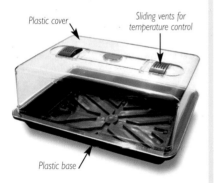

Plastic cover

Sliding vents for temperature control

Plastic base

Propagators are one step on from the old sheet of glass over a tray method. In essence, they comprise a coloured plastic base and a clear plastic cover – a bit like a miniature greenhouse. The pot-sown seedlings are simply placed in the propagator, and sunlight or a small electrical heater does the rest.

SOWING AND PLANTING IN THE GROUND

Scattering seeds Small seeds, like those of carrots, can be sown as a pinch, or mixed with dry silver sand and dribbled. Aim for a coverage that suits the final spacing.

Planting seeds Seeds like those of peas and even beetroot are large enough to handle individually. They can be spaced in a wide shallow drill, or set into holes.

Onion sets Onion sets (small immature bulbs) are pushed into the earth so that the tip is just showing above the soil.

Potatoes Potato seeds can be dropped into large dibbed or dug holes, or set into a wide drill. They can be earthed up little by little, or all in one go.

Make a shallow V-section drill and dribble the seeds into it

Make a wide, shallow drill – a trench – and place each seed by hand

Push onion sets gently into the correct position

Earth up potatoes so that the shoots are covered

THINNING

The object of thinning is to finish up with the best seedlings at the correct spacing. The initial sowing density can be adjusted to suit the predicted fertility and the final spacing. If you have a plant with a good fertility record – say beetroot – it pays to be really mean for the initial spacing.

TRANSPLANTING

Transplanting involves lifting the fragile seedling and setting it into its final growing space. Plants such as cabbages can be lifted by the trowel-full, teased apart and then planted. Plants such as tomatoes are best planted in pockets or fibre pots so that the transplanting can be achieved with the minimum of root damage.

A–Z of growing vegetables

Every day, it seems, another newspaper article tells us about the dangers of eating poor-quality shop-bought food and the benefits of growing and eating our own. It is sad to think that some children have never tasted a freshly pulled carrot or a handful of peas straight from the pod. The good news is that the whole idea of growing vegetables is rapidly growing in popularity – now just about everyone knows that it is the best way forward.

An untidy but healthy mix of greens, radishes and carrots, which are all growing well and are set to produce a good crop.

You need to know

- A good look around your allotment will show you that the site and soil are good for some vegetables and not so good for others. For example, it might be just right for growing root crops and not so good for sweetcorn. Be ready to change your planting list accordingly, and be aware that some crops are easier to grow than others.

- If this book says 'sow in April' and you see that your neighbouring holders are all sowing the same crop in March, try a row or two in April, but be ready to follow their lead next time around and sow that bit earlier. In short, sowing and planting times can vary according to local conditions.

- Plant care, including feeding, watering and control of weeds, pests and diseases, is a vital ingredient for success on an allotment. Never neglect any of these tasks.

- A productive plot is rarely neat and tidy. Look and learn from the plot-holder who is busy cropping a little bit of this and a little bit of that when everyone else has tidied up in readiness for winter.

GETTING STARTED

It is always best to start by growing the basics: the simple, ordinary crops such as cabbages, runner beans and potatoes, and then take it from there. Do not try to dig the whole plot in the first season, and, most importantly, do not think that there are any significant shortcuts. Like everything else that is worth doing, you have to start little and work big. Have a good long look at the seed catalogue, ask neighbouring allotment-holders about all the dos, don'ts and what-withs, and then gently go your own way.

Do not try to double dig the whole allotment in the first season. Plan out the overall shape of the plot, decide where you want the shed, cover up most of the ground with old carpet or black plastic to kill off the weeds, and then build the shed and start digging the first plot. It is a good morale-booster to select the vegetables that you have always wanted to grow. I wanted to grow the biggest and best runner beans. We finished up with enough runner beans to feed a small army, and we discovered that there is nothing quite like working all day on the allotment and then eating a plate of fresh beans – day after day – but it was such pleasure!

GOING ORGANIC

Most people would probably now agree that organic is the best, perhaps the only, way to proceed – after all, who wants to eat something that is less than perfect, or something that has been dipped and doused in poisonous chemicals? To my way of thinking, however, you have no choice other than to take things slowly. You could start by never using chemicals – no weedkillers, no sprays. You could then go on to using organic manures. It is not easy, because your horse manure might come from a stable where there are sick horses that are being pumped full of chemicals and drugs, or horses that are fed on non-organic fodder. Of course, what goes in one end of a horse will eventually come out at the other. Then again, a load of horse manure has got to be better than a cartload of artificial fertilizers.

So it goes on. What can you do about the gardener on the neighbouring allotment who wants to spray the whole world with chemicals? Some allotments are actively pushing towards being totally organic. You could perhaps try to push your allotment in that direction. It will be an uphill struggle, but just do your best.

Globe artichokes

If you are looking to fill a small corner of the allotment, you enjoy experimenting with exotic vegetables and you consider yourself to be something of a gourmet, then this unusual, prickly-looking plant is a good one to choose. It should impress your dinner guests!

			SOW	PLANT			HARVEST																
Jan	Feb	Mar	Apr	May	Jun	Jul	Aug	Sep	Oct	Nov	Dec	Jan	Feb	Mar	Apr	May	Jun	Jul	Aug	Sep	Oct	Nov	Dec

Green Globe
Second only to Purple Globe, this is the one that you are most likely to see on the allotment. It has dark green heads with attractive foliage, and is best obtained from specialist nurseries.

More varieties
- **Purple Globe – Romanesco:** Purple to red flower buds. It is slightly smaller than Green Globe, and does well in long, cold winters. If you live in a cold, windy area, then this is a good choice. A swift allotment survey suggests that, of all the varieties, this is the one most growers choose.

- **Violetta di Chioggia:** A variety known as much for its beautiful purple-headed good looks as for its taste. It is, more often than not, listed as a decorative plant for the flower borders, rather than a vegetable. This is the one that beginners to allotments sometimes cut and destroy, mistakenly thinking that it is the much-dreaded giant thistle.

SOIL AND SITE NEEDS

The globe artichoke does best in a deep rich soil with full exposure to sunlight. It needs plenty of moisture throughout the summer months, and a well-drained soil during the winter. Traditionally it was grown in beds. A good method is to plant one or more plants a year for four years – say 1, 2, 3 and 4 – and then to remove and replace plant(s) 1 in year five, and so on. In this way, you will always have a succession of good cropping plants. The primary needs are a generous dressing of well-rotted farmyard manure – spread and dug in during the spring and autumn – and plenty of moisture.

SOWING AND PLANTING PROCEDURES

- Although artichokes can be sown from seed, the easiest and most common option is to propagate from tubers or root suckers.
- April – plant the suckers singly about 10 cm (4 in) deep, with 60 cm (2 ft) between plants and 75 cm (30 in) between rows.
- Tread the plants in well and water them generously.
- Water daily and provide shade, until the plant looks to be well established.

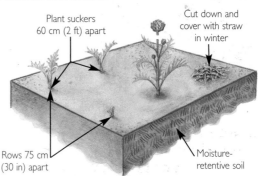

Plant suckers 60 cm (2 ft) apart

Cut down and cover with straw in winter

Rows 75 cm (30 in) apart

Moisture-retentive soil

PLANT CARE

In the summer, stir the ground with the hoe to keep it loose-mulched and clean. Water and mulch. In the first season, cut and discard the heads. In the winter, cut the foliage down to the ground and cover the crowns with straw. In the second season, remove the straw, and apply fertilizer/manure in the spring.

HARVESTING

Harvest from late June onwards, when the heads are mature but the scales still closed. Cut them off with 5–7.5 cm (2–3 in) of stem. Stand them in water until needed. After the first crop, cut the stems down and allow the new suckers to produce a late crop.

TROUBLESHOOTING

- **Slugs** Set slug traps, and gather the slugs by hand.
- **Aphids** The moment you see the aphids, pinch out affected areas and spray with a solution of water and liquid soap. Stir the ground around the stems to encourage aphid-eating predators.
- **Blotched brown heads** Likely to be petal blight, a fungus that affects the heads and flowers. Pick and burn the heads.

Asparagus

■ ■he good news is that asparagus is fast becoming one of our most popular vegetables. You might have to wait 3–4 years before you get a really good, piled-high plateful, but it is a tasty treat that is well worth waiting for. If you grow from one-year-old crowns, you can crop in two years.

SOW	PLANT																						
Jan	Feb	Mar	Apr	May	Jun	Jul	Aug	Sep	Oct	Nov	Dec	Jan	Feb	Mar	Apr	May	Jun	Jul	Aug	Sep	Oct	Nov	Dec

Year 2-3

				HARVEST																			
Jan	Feb	Mar	Apr	May	Jun	Jul	Aug	Sep	Oct	Nov	Dec	Jan	Feb	Mar	Apr	May	Jun	Jul	Aug	Sep	Oct	Nov	Dec

Connovers Colossal

A long-established variety that has proven its worth over the years, and has thick, mid- to light green stalks. Asparagus aficionados say that a well-looked-after bed of this variety will crop well for 15–20 years.

More varieties

- **Early Purple Argenteuil:** Although this is the variety that many growers favour as being reliable, and as tasty as Connovers Colossal, it is now rather difficult to find in the catalogues.

- **F1 Jersey Knight:** An all-male, disease-resistant hybrid that produces good fat spears.

- **Mary Washington:** A rust-resistant variety particularly recommended as suitable for allotment and home garden growers. It produces an abundance of long, straight, thick and heavy, dark green to purple spears.

SOIL AND SITE NEEDS

Asparagus does best in a well-drained, deep, rich soil that is inclined to be sandy, in a sheltered but sunny spot. The ground should be deeply dug and well prepared. Traditionally, it was thought that the plants thrived when the soil was enriched with 15–30 tons of well-rotted farmyard manure to the acre – say, a couple of buckets every square metre (yard). During the season, gently stir or hoe the soil to open it up and keep it free from weeds.

SOWING AND PLANTING PROCEDURES

- Dig a trench 25 cm (10 in) deep and 38 cm (15 in) wide. Cover the base with 7.5 cm (3 in) of gently mounded compost or well-rotted manure.
- Mid-March to end April – set the crowns 45 cm (18 in) apart, with their roots spread over the mound, and cover them with 5–7.5 cm (2–3 in) of soil. Water them generously.

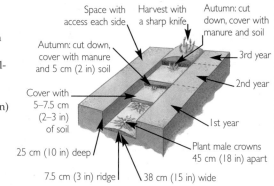

Space with access each side / Harvest with a sharp knife / Autumn: cut down, cover with manure and soil / 3rd year / Autumn: cut down, cover with manure and 5 cm (2 in) soil / 2nd year / Cover with 5–7.5 cm (2–3 in) of soil / 1st year / 25 cm (10 in) deep / 7.5 cm (3 in) ridge / 38 cm (15 in) wide / Plant male crowns 45 cm (18 in) apart

PLANT CARE

In the first and second autumn after planting, before the berries have a chance to develop, cut the foliage, stir the surface with the hoe to provide a loose-soil mulch, and cover with well-rotted manure topped with soil. In the third autumn after planting, and in all future years, repeat the procedure, but let the spears grow. Rake off loose soil in spring and apply fertilizer.

HARVESTING

You can harvest from mid-April to late June. In the third season, when the spears have pushed 7.5–10 cm (3–4 in) above ground, take a long-bladed knife and slide the blade at a flat angle into the soil to sever the spear at a point 7.5–10 cm (3–4 in) below ground level.

TROUBLESHOOTING

- **Slugs** Set slug traps, and gather the slugs by hand.
- **Roots dying off** Likely to be a fungus called violet root rot. Burn all the affected plants, and start again with fresh stock on a fresh bed.
- **Blackened stems** Probably frost damage. Cut away affected shoots and protect from frost.

Aubergines (eggplants)

Much loved by our European neighbours, the aubergine is now at last being grown on allotments around the UK. Grown as much to impress as to eat, this is the perfect choice for tomato-growers who are looking for a new challenge, as aubergines are grown from seed just like tomatoes.

SOW	PLANT		HARVEST																				
Jan	Feb	Mar	Apr	May	Jun	Jul	Aug	Sep	Oct	Nov	Dec	Jan	Feb	Mar	Apr	May	Jun	Jul	Aug	Sep	Oct	Nov	Dec

Long Purple

A traditional, medium-early variety that produces long, shiny, violet-coloured fruit at an average length of about 13–15 cm (5–6 in).
It is a good choice for beginners.

More varieties

- **Black Enorma:** A variety grown primarily for the size of its fruits. Some growers feel that the enormous size is offset by the mild flavour.

- **F1 Long Tom:** A high-yielding variety, sometimes producing a bumper crop of 25–30 fruits per plant. It produces black to purple fruits about 13–15 cm (5–6 in) long.

- **F1 Money Maker:** A productive, extra-early variety with smooth, glossy, black, medium-long fruits.

- **Snowy:** An early-maturing variety, and a good choice in an area with short, wet summers. It has long, cylindrical, white fruits about 18–20 cm (7–8 in) long. It is easy to grow and very tasty, with a smooth, glossy, firm, white skin.

SOIL AND SITE NEEDS

The aubergine (eggplant) does best in a deep, well-drained, fertile soil in a sunny, sheltered position. It does not like frost, waterlogged soil or sharp winds. Traditionally, gardeners recommended digging in leafmould. A good modern option is to grow them in 23 cm (9 in) pots filled with potting compost, or in growing-bags (two plants to the bag) in much the same way as indoor tomatoes. Provide each plant with its own little individual plastic-sheet shelter (a large cloche or a polytunnel) or build a plastic screen to the windward side (something like a canvas beach screen).

SOWING AND PLANTING PROCEDURES

- March – sow the seeds in a tray on a bed of moistened potting compost, and protect them with a sheet of glass covered with newspaper. Keep the tray warm.
- April–May – when the seedlings are large enough, prick them out into 7.5 cm (3 in) peat pots. Water and keep them warm.
- April–May – place the peat pots in 23 cm (9 in) pots, water generously and protect with the cloche or plastic shelter of your choice.

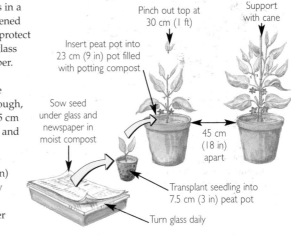

Pinch out top at 30 cm (1 ft)

Support with cane

Insert peat pot into 23 cm (9 in) pot filled with potting compost

Sow seed under glass and newspaper in moist compost

45 cm (18 in) apart

Transplant seedling into 7.5 cm (3 in) peat pot

Turn glass daily

PLANT CARE

Water frequently. When the plant is about 30 cm (1 ft) high, remove the growing tip to encourage branching. Support with a cane and ties. Pinch out to leave the best six fruits, and remove subsequent flowers. Spray with water to discourage aphids. Apply a liquid feed, and strip off the older foliage.

HARVESTING

Depending on the variety, where you live and your growing methods, you can harvest from late July to mid-October. When the fruits are 15–23 cm (6–9 in) long and nicely plump and shiny, slice them off with a sharp knife.

TROUBLESHOOTING

- **Aphids, red spider mites, whitefly** Spray with a water and liquid soap solution, and wash the leaves with plain water.
- **Withered, wilted or split fruits** Sometimes caused by heavy watering after drought-wet-drought conditions. The answer is to keep the soil moist rather than 'puddle', by covering the ground with a mulch of well-rotted manure.

Broad beans

Growing broad beans can be a challenge but, if the pleasure of removing the plump beans from their fur-lined pods does not make it all worthwhile, then a plate of steamed beans served up with a chunk of buttered brown bread should do the trick.

| Jan | Feb | Mar | Apr | May | Jun | Jul | Aug | Sep | Oct | Nov | Dec | Jan | Feb | Mar | Apr | May | Jun | Jul | Aug | Sep | Oct | Nov | Dec |

SOW | **HARVEST** | **SOW (WINTER CROP)** | **HARVEST (WINTER CROP)**

Bunyards Exhibition

An English heirloom variety that has been popular ever since it was introduced way back in the 1880s. It produces a heavy crop with 9–10 long pods, and has a good, strong flavour. It freezes well.

More varieties

- **Dreadnought:** A swift-growing variety. It produces good-sized pods with large, white beans. The flavour is excellent and it freezes well.

- **Green Windsor:** A traditional variety related to the much-favoured Broad Windsor. All the Windsor types have short pods and lots of flavour.

- **Masterpiece Green:** A tried-and-trusted favourite with growers and cooks alike, an early variety that produces an abundance of long pods with bright green beans. Good choice if you enjoy whole platefuls of beans.

- **Witkiem Manita:** A superior early variety – just right to sow in autumn. It produces 5–7 good pods, 18–20 cm (7–8 in) long.

SOIL AND SITE NEEDS

Broad beans will grow in almost any kind of soil, but they do best in a deep, rich, moisture-retentive soil that has been enriched with well-rotted farmyard manure. Experienced growers recommend a light, well-drained soil for earlies (meaning beans that are sown in November and cropped in June of the following season) and a heavier soil for the main crop that is sown between January and May and cropped from June of the same year. As a general guide, broad beans like a sunny, sheltered spot with a moist, well-drained soil, and dislike draughts and waterlogged heavy soil.

SOWING AND PLANTING PROCEDURES

- February–April – for the main crop, in sandy soil, prepare 7.5 cm (3 in) deep drills (in heavy soil, prepare 7.5 cm (3 in) deep dibbed holes); sow single seeds 13–20 cm (5–8 in) apart in rows 45 cm (18 in) apart. Water.
- Winter-hardy crop – throughout November, sow in 7.5 cm (3 in) deep drills or dibbed holes, as above.
- Water generously and make the seed bed firm.

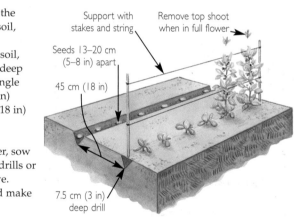

Support with stakes and string

Remove top shoot when in full flower

Seeds 13–20 cm (5–8 in) apart

45 cm (18 in)

7.5 cm (3 in) deep drill

PLANT CARE

When the plants are a few centimetres (inches) high, draw the soil around the stems. Stir the soil with a hoe to provide a loose soil mulch and to keep it clean. As soon as the blooms are set, pinch out and destroy the top shoots; this will plump up the pods and hold back the blackfly. After flowering, water frequently. Support with stakes and string.

HARVESTING

You can harvest between late June and October – the date depends on the variety and the planting date. When the beans are firm, tweak the pods from the stem. When the crop is finished, cut the plant down to the ground to leave the root in the soil.

TROUBLESHOOTING

- **Blackfly** Pinch out and remove affected areas, and spray with a solution of water and liquid soap.
- **Blotchy brown-yellow leaves** Probably halo blight. Lift and burn diseased plants. Do not plant on the same plot the next time around.
- **Nibbles and notches** Nibbles around the edges of tender leaves are caused by the bean weevil. Avoid the problem by hoeing around the young plants.

French beans

If you enjoy eating beans, French beans are very useful in that they extend the season by being on your plate 2–3 weeks before runner beans are available. If you are really keen and plant them under cover, you can harvest them in mid-June. French beans are good if you are short of space.

| Jan | Feb | Mar | Apr | May | Jun | Jul | Aug | Sep | Oct | Nov | Dec | Jan | Feb | Mar | Apr | May | Jun | Jul | Aug | Sep | Oct | Nov | Dec |

Sungold
A slightly unusual-looking variety that produces lots of slender, bright yellow beans. There are many varieties to choose from, but if you want to brighten up your plate this is a good option.

More varieties

- **Barlotta Lingua di Fuoco:** A swift-growing, climbing variety that bears lots of green-pink pods. It is good fun to grow and eat – the pink colour turns to green on cooking.

- **Canadian Wonder:** A traditional variety that has been around since the early 1900s. It produces a heavy crop of long, flat, bright green pods, which have a good flavour and tender texture when picked young.

- **Masterpiece:** A good choice for an early crop. It has a large, long, flat, green pod, like a short runner bean.

- **Safari:** A late-maturing, disease-resistant variety, sometimes sold as 'Kenyan'. It produces dark green, round-section, stringless pods.

SOIL AND SITE NEEDS

Although ideally French beans do best on a light soil, just about any well-manured, well-prepared soil will yield a fair crop. Do not use fresh manure. A good set-up is ground that has been deeply worked and heavily manured for a previous crop. Give a light dressing of lime before the seeds are sown. As soon as the plants are up and growing, spread a mulch of old manure alongside the rows. French beans need a sunny, sheltered spot well away from gusty winds and draughts. They must be protected against frosts and driving rain.

SOWING AND PLANTING PROCEDURES

- April–May – for an early crop, prepare 5 cm (2 in) deep drills, and sow the seeds 5–7.5 cm (2–3 in) apart, in rows 45 cm (18 in) apart.
- May–June – for the main crop, sow as above.
- June–July – sow as above.
- Water generously.
- Early and late crops will need to be protected with cloches or polytunnels.

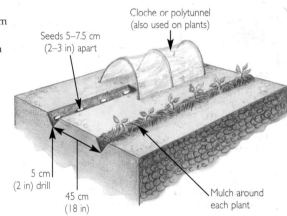

Cloche or polytunnel (also used on plants)

Seeds 5–7.5 cm (2–3 in) apart

5 cm (2 in) drill

45 cm (18 in)

Mulch around each plant

PLANT CARE

When the plants are a few centimetres (inches) high, draw the soil around the stems to protect them against frost and draughts. Stir with a hoe to provide a loose-soil mulch and to keep the soil clean, and mulch with old spent manure or peat. Water generously at the roots, but keep it away from the foliage. Support climbing varieties.

HARVESTING

You can start picking from July onwards, the time depending on the variety and the planting date. When the beans are firm within the pod, give the pods a good twist so that they come off cleanly.

TROUBLESHOOTING

- **Blackfly** More common with broad beans. Pinch out and remove affected areas, and repeatedly spray with a solution of water and liquid soap.
- **Wilting stems** Pull and burn the plants and go for a disease-resistant variety the next time around.
- **Blotchy brown-yellow leaves** Probably halo blight. Pull and burn diseased plants, and avoid planting French beans on the same plot for a couple of years.

Runner beans

The good old runner bean is one of most people's favourite vegetables – we enjoy growing them, it is good fun building the supports, they are beautifully decorative when they are growing, they crop well, they have a long growing season and, best of all, they taste absolutely delicious!

Jan	Feb	Mar	Apr	May	Jun	Jul	Aug	Sep	Oct	Nov	Dec	Jan	Feb	Mar	Apr	May	Jun	Jul	Aug	Sep	Oct	Nov	Dec

SOW — May/Jun   HARVEST — Aug/Sep

Prizewinner
A well-known and popular prize-winning variety. Produces long, straight, dark to mid-green pods. If Scarlet Emperor and Red Rum are your first two choices, then let Prizewinner be your third.

Red Rum
A heavy-cropping, disease-resistant variety. Produces narrow, straight beans about 15–20 cm (6–8 in) in length. This is a good option if you cannot get hold of Scarlet Emperor. Very tasty.

Scarlet Emperor
A tried-and-trusted old favourite that has been around at least since the beginning of the twentieth century. Produces a long, rough-textured bean, with a flavour and texture that cannot be beaten. The perfect runner bean.

More varieties
- **Keledon Wonder:** Well-known, early variety that produces pairs of short pods. It has a good, strong flavour.

- **Painted Lady:** It is amazing to think that this variety has been around for at least 150 years and is still going strong. It is a winner on many counts: it is easy to grow, the plant is splendidly decorative – the red and white flowers are a picture – it produces masses of pods and the taste and texture are mouth-watering.

- **Streamline:** Well-known, reliable variety that produces a heavy crop of dark green, rough-textured pods. A good choice if you like Scarlet Emperor but are looking for a slightly softer texture and a milder flavour.

SOIL AND SITE NEEDS

Although runner beans thrive in any well-prepared allotment soil, a medium to light loam is the ideal. Clay soils are just about acceptable if they are open and well drained, but overall they are least suitable. If you are after a heavy crop, it is a good idea to dig in lots of well-rotted farmyard manure.

A good option is to dig a 60 cm (2 ft) wide, 23 cm (9 in) deep trench in the autumn and use it as a compost pit. If your site is generally quite windy and exposed, plant two rows about 1.2 m (4 ft) apart and either 'dwarf' the plant by picking out the top flowers as soon as they show, or better still build a super-strong A-frame tunnel and leave the beans to it. Most runner-bean enthusiasts will opt for building a permanent frame from something such as mild steel angle iron and plastic mesh.

SOWING AND PLANTING PROCEDURES

- Prepare the trench – as early in the year as conditions allow – 60 cm (2 ft) wide and 23 cm (9 in) deep. Fill it with rotted manure topped with soil.
- Build the support frame.
- To raise runner-bean seedlings under glass in April or May, plant seeds in compost-filled pots.
- Plant the seedlings out at the end of May. Set them at 15 cm (6 in) intervals along the prepared trench.
- To sow seeds directly in the ground in May or June, run 5 cm (2 in) deep drills along the trench and sow the seeds 13–15 cm (5–6 in) apart.

SOWING AND PLANTING PROCEDURES (CONTINUED)

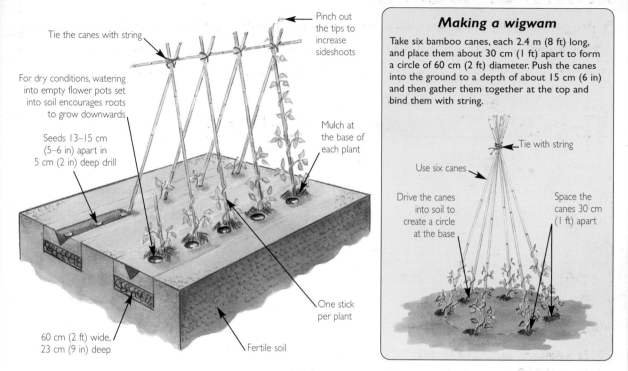

Tie the canes with string

Pinch out the tips to increase sideshoots

For dry conditions, watering into empty flower pots set into soil encourages roots to grow downwards

Seeds 13–15 cm (5–6 in) apart in 5 cm (2 in) deep drill

Mulch at the base of each plant

60 cm (2 ft) wide, 23 cm (9 in) deep

One stick per plant

Fertile soil

Making a wigwam

Take six bamboo canes, each 2.4 m (8 ft) long, and place them about 30 cm (1 ft) apart to form a circle of 60 cm (2 ft) diameter. Push the canes into the ground to a depth of about 15 cm (6 in) and then gather them together at the top and bind them with string.

Tie with string

Use six canes

Drive the canes into soil to create a circle at the base

Space the canes 30 cm (1 ft) apart

PLANT CARE

Stir the soil with a hoe to create a loose-soil mulch and to keep it clean. In very dry weather, spread a mulch of straw or old manure at either side of the row to help hold in moisture. Some growers bury empty flower pots in the soil for easy watering, the thinking being that the pots directly target the water at the roots. Some growers favour spraying the plants in the evening just before the sun goes down. Pinch out the tips as soon as they reach the top of the frame. Encourage growth by removing old pods. Make sure all along the way that the supports are secure.

TROUBLESHOOTING

← Aphids *Large colonies of aphids can be a real nuisance to the extent that they generally stunt growth. Pinch out and remove affected areas and spray with a mix of water and liquid soap.*

↙ Bean weevil *Shows itself as nibbles and notches around the edges of tender leaves. The best way of solving the problem is to prevent it from happening, by hoeing around the young plants when they are at the two- or three-leaf stage.*

↙ Halo blight *Shows itself as yellow-edged brown blotches on the leaves, resulting in a low yield. Lift and burn diseased plants. Do not plant on the same plot the next time around.*

Other troubles *Although they can sometimes be affected by mildew, seed flies, birds, worms, moths, bugs and other pests, runner beans are wonderfully trouble-free plants. A common problem, however, is pod wither, which can often be prevented simply by giving the plants lots of water at the flowering stage.*

HARVESTING

You can harvest from July through to October. Pick when the pods are young and slender, just at the point when the shape of the beans within the pod begins to show. The more you pick, the more you will get. The secret is to pick as often as possible. Don't wait until the weekend; try to pick every evening. Be aware that if you allow the pods to grow to maturity the plant will come to a halt. Search out any old, overgrown, tough pods and throw them away.

Harvesting caution

Some people are touch-sensitive to fine hairs on runner-bean plants – their skin comes up in a rash. If you are worried about this, then wear a long-sleeved shirt to protect your arms, cotton gloves and a silk or cotton scarf around your neck.

Beet leaf

Known variously as spinach beet, perpetual spinach, chard and one or two other names, beet leaf is a good choice if you have not had much luck growing spinach. It has a much stronger flavour than spinach, but it can be grown all year round.

			SOW					HARVEST															
Jan	Feb	Mar	Apr	May	Jun	Jul	Aug	Sep	Oct	Nov	Dec	Jan	Feb	Mar	Apr	May	Jun	Jul	Aug	Sep	Oct	Nov	Dec

Swiss Chard

Sometimes called Beet Chard or even Seakale Beet, this variety produces dark glossy leaves on long, white, celery-like stems. The stems can be steamed, just like celery.

More varieties

- **Perpetual Spinach:** A great easy-to-grow variety that produces light green leaves on thin green stems – it keeps going for most of the year.

- **Rainbow:** A very attractive plant that produces masses of dark green leaves on yellow to red-orange stems. Everything can be eaten.

- **Rhubarb Chard:** It looks a bit like young rhubarb. Everything can be eaten – the leaves like spinach, and the stems steamed, like asparagus.

- **Yellow Chard:** A well-known, easy-to-grow variety with bright green, fleshy leaves on yellow stems. The leaves can be steamed, like spinach, and the young tender stalks can be eaten like celery.

SOIL AND SITE NEEDS

Beet leaf has more or less the same needs as spinach, meaning it likes well-manured, deeply dug soil in a sunny position. While beet leaf can be grown on poorer soil in a more exposed position than ordinary spinach, it will really thrive if the soil is rich. The soil needs to be moist but well-drained. Some growers favour planting the crop in raised beds about 1.2–1.5 m (4–5 ft) wide. The idea is that rainwater can pass away quickly and the crop can be gathered without the need to tread on the soil.

SOWING AND PLANTING PROCEDURES

- Mid-March–mid-May – create 18 mm (¾ in) deep drills 38 cm (15 in) apart, and sow a group of 3–4 seeds at 23 cm (9 in) intervals.
- Compact the soil and water generously with a fine spray.
- When the seedlings are big enough to handle, pinch some out to leave only the strongest plant in each group.
- Compact and firm up the soil around the plants.

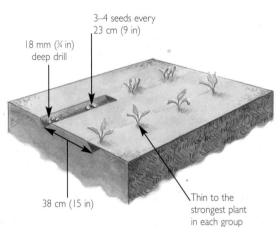

3–4 seeds every 23 cm (9 in)

18 mm (¾ in) deep drill

38 cm (15 in)

Thin to the strongest plant in each group

PLANT CARE

Stir the soil with a hoe to create a loose-soil mulch and to keep it free from weeds. If the weather is very dry, you could spread a mulch of old manure around the plants to hold in the moisture. Water generously in dry spells. Remove flowers, damaged stalks and leaves, and plants that bolt.

HARVESTING

You can harvest from July right the way round to the following June – the date depending on the variety, where you live and how much protection you give the plants. Pick young leaves close to the ground. Keep the plant healthy by picking off old and yellow leaves.

TROUBLESHOOTING

- **Split roots** Usually caused by long spells of dry weather. You can prevent the problem by covering the ground with a deep mulch of spent manure.
- **Bolting** Caused by drought. Mulch with spent manure, be generous with the water, and use bolt-resistant varieties next time.
- **Slugs** Set slug traps, and gather the slugs by hand.

Beetroot

Attractive in colour, sweet in taste, firm but juicy in texture, and wonderfully easy to grow, beetroot (sometimes known as beet) has long been thought of as the perfect companion to salads; it can also be eaten as a hot vegetable served with meat.

SOW		HARVEST																					
Jan	Feb	Mar	Apr	May	Jun	Jul	Aug	Sep	Oct	Nov	Dec	Jan	Feb	Mar	Apr	May	Jun	Jul	Aug	Sep	Oct	Nov	Dec

Tardel

A good variety for late sowing up to early June. It produces firm, sweet and tasty, globe-shaped baby beetroots, perfect for salads. The flavour and texture are beautiful.

More varieties

- **Cheltenham Green Top:** A tried-and-trusted, traditional variety that has been around for at least a century. It produces long, tapering roots with good texture and flavour.

- **Crimson King:** A choice variety that produces medium to large, round roots, perfect for storing, with a firm texture and delicate flavour.

- **Detroit:** A choice variety that has been around for almost a century. It produces solid roots that are good for storing. The deep red flesh has a characteristic flavour.

- **Mammoth Long:** A good, reliable, easy-to-grow variety. It produces long, smooth, cylindrical roots. The flesh is dark, firm and sweet.

SOIL AND SITE NEEDS

Beetroot can be grown on just about any ordinary allotment soil, but a light, sandy soil produces the best-shaped roots. It can be grown on clay, as long as it is deeply dug and well worked, and ridged in winter to encourage maximum break-up. Traditionally, growers on clay soils sowed a couple of weeks later than the usual time, the idea being that it would keep the roots small and compact rather than large and coarse. The ground needs to be well drained and well manured, but at the same time the manure must not be fresh or rank. It is much better if beetroot is planted on fertile soil that has been manured for a preceding crop.

SOWING AND PLANTING PROCEDURES

- Early March–late June – create 2.5 cm (1 in) deep drills 25–30 cm (10–12 in) apart, and sow a group of 3–4 seeds (ready-soaked in water for one hour) at 13 cm (5 in) intervals.
- Compact the soil and water generously.
- When the seedlings are big enough to handle, carefully pinch them out to leave the strongest plant in each group.
- Firm the soil up around the stems of the remaining plants, and water generously with a fine spray.

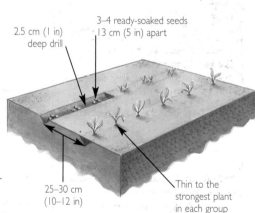

2.5 cm (1 in) deep drill

3–4 ready-soaked seeds 13 cm (5 in) apart

25–30 cm (10–12 in)

Thin to the strongest plant in each group

PLANT CARE

Spread a web of black cotton thread over the young plants to keep off birds. Thin out to the strongest plant in each group and use the baby beet for salad. Stir the soil with a hoe to create a loose-soil mulch and to keep it clean. In dry weather, spread a mulch of spent manure to hold in the moisture, and water frequently.

HARVESTING

You can harvest from May to November – the date depending on the variety and growing methods. Use a fork to ease the root from the ground. Twist the leaves off about 5 cm (2 in) above the crown, and eat fresh, or store in sand.

TROUBLESHOOTING

- **Split roots** Usually caused by long spells of dry weather. Avoid this problem by covering the ground with a deep mulch of spent manure.
- **Bolting** Caused by drought. Mulch with spent manure or chopped straw, be generous with the water, and use bolt-resistant varieties.
- **Slugs** Set slug traps, and gather the slugs by hand.

Broccoli

Sprouting broccoli, white and purple, is one of the tastiest cut-and-come-again vegetables. If you sow successive varieties and harvest with care, you can, with a break in June, be eating broccoli spears and flowers from late January to late October.

| SOW | PLANT | | | | | | HARVEST (Depends on variety) | HARVEST |
| Jan | Feb | Mar | Apr | May | Jun | Jul | Aug | Sep | Oct | Nov | Dec | Jan | Feb | Mar | Apr | May | Jun | Jul | Aug | Sep | Oct | Nov | Dec |

Red Arrow

A good purple variety for cropping in March and April. It produces an abundance of characteristic bright purple flowers or spears with a firm texture and medium to strong taste.

More varieties

• **Purple Sprouting Early:** It bears a wealth of dark purple spears in March. Pick the spears when they are young and tender, with a beautifully firm texture and tangy taste.

• **Purple Sprouting Late**: Much the same as the purple sprouting early variety, the only difference being that it can be cropped from April onwards.

• **Waltham:** A green calabrese-type variety with a central head followed by an abundance of sideshoots.

• **White Sprouting Early:** A very popular and reliable white variety. It produces white spears from late February–March and onwards. The flavour is milder and a bit less distinct than that of purple varieties.

SOIL AND SITE NEEDS

Broccoli can be grown on a sandy soil, but it does best on a heavy, fertile loam that is inclined to clay. The soil should be well manured and compact, and deeply dug for a previous crop – with plenty of moisture-retentive organic matter. If you have built raised beds on a difficult-to-work clay soil, this is one of those times when you can plant out in the clay. Experienced growers say that well-cultivated, compact soil equates with good-looking compact heads on the broccoli, while loose, over-rich soil is likely to produce scraggy, open heads. Try if possible to plant in a spot that is open and sunny without being windy.

SOWING AND PLANTING PROCEDURES

• April–May – sow seeds in a prepared seed bed or in seed-trays.
• June–July – planting out is best done on a dull rainy day, so that you do not have to water.
• Dib holes 45–70 cm (18–27 in) apart, with 45–70 cm (18–27 in) between rows. Use lots of water to 'puddle' the seedlings into the holes.
• Use your fingers to compact the soil around the plants.

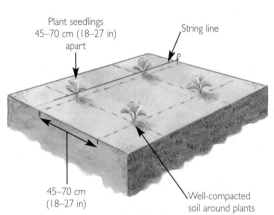

Plant seedlings 45–70 cm (18–27 in) apart

String line

45–70 cm (18–27 in)

Well-compacted soil around plants

PLANT CARE

Water the seedlings before and after planting, and then daily. Stir the surface soil with a hoe to create a loose-soil mulch and to keep it clean. In dry weather, spread a mulch of spent manure to hold in the moisture. If you have applied fertilizer for a previous crop, you can give it a miss for the broccoli.

HARVESTING

You can harvest from January to May, and July to November – depending on the variety and how much protection you give the plants. Start by picking the central spear or head, and follow up by picking the little sideshoots. Pick every few days to encourage new growth.

TROUBLESHOOTING

• **Caterpillars** Remove the caterpillars by hand. Keep the white butterflies at bay by covering the crop with a fine net.
• **Pigeons** Protect the crop with a mess of fine cottons, or cover with a net.
• **Sticky distorted leaves** Can be caused by aphids and whitefly. Spray the plants with a solution of water and liquid soap.

Brussels sprouts

Everyone hates sprouts when they are boiled down to a gross green gruel, but when they are served up firm and tight with a dab of butter or a dash of olive oil, and a sprinkling of fresh ground black pepper, they are simply delicious.

	SOW		PLANT						HARVEST														
Jan	Feb	Mar	Apr	May	Jun	Jul	Aug	Sep	Oct	Nov	Dec	Jan	Feb	Mar	Apr	May	Jun	Jul	Aug	Sep	Oct	Nov	Dec

FI Oliver

A very early, disease-resistant variety that crops from August right through to October. It produces masses of large, medium green sprouts with a good strong flavour – everything you would expect of a sprout.

More varieties

- **Early Half Tall:** The low, dwarfing habit of this variety makes it a good choice for an exposed, windy plot.

- **Evesham Special:** A dependable, traditional variety that has masses of tight, firm, medium-sized sprouts from September to December.

- **FI Igor:** A vigorous, frost-resistant, high-yielding variety that produces masses of tight, round sprouts with a good, strong flavour.

- **Rubine:** A variety that crops from December to February. It produces large, red-purple sprouts.

- **Trafalgar:** A new tall, mid-season variety that produces an abundance of small to medium-sized, firm sprouts.

SOIL AND SITE NEEDS

Brussels sprouts do best in a deeply worked, rich, fertile, firm soil in a plot that allows for a long season of growth, with the emphasis on deeply worked and firm. They do not like to be packed into a small space and they do not like a loose soil. So be warned – if the soil is overly rich and loose, the plants will shake about in the ground, resulting in loose, open sprouts. The best advice is to manure and dig for a preceding crop and then to plant out the sprouts. Ideally, the plot needs to be sunny and open and yet free from winds. If your plot is generally windy, choose compact, low-growing varieties.

SOWING AND PLANTING PROCEDURES

- March–April -- sow seeds in a prepared seed bed or in seed-trays.
- May–early June – planting out is best done on a dull, rainy day so that you do not have to water.
- Firm the ground with the back of a spade or with a roller. Dib holes 50–90 cm (20–36 in) apart, with 50–90 cm (20–36 in) between rows. 'Puddle' the seedlings into the holes until the lowest leaf is at soil level, and use your fingers to firm up the soil around the plants to prevent wind damage in autumn.

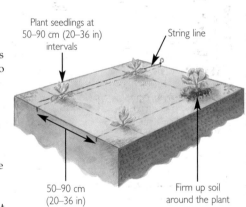

Plant seedlings at 50–90 cm (20–36 in) intervals

String line

50–90 cm (20–36 in)

Firm up soil around the plant

PLANT CARE

Water the seedlings before and after planting, and then daily. Stir the surface of the soil with a hoe to create a loose-soil mulch and to keep it clean. Remove the bottom leaves as they become yellow. Spread a mulch of spent manure or straw over the loose soil to hold in the moisture. Firm up the soil in the autumn.

HARVESTING

You can harvest from September to March – the date depending on the variety and growing methods. Work from bottom to top up the stem, picking only the best tight sprouts. Put tired sprouts and yellow leaves on the compost heap.

TROUBLESHOOTING

- **Holes in leaves** Caused by caterpillars and birds. Avoid the problem by growing the sprouts in a netted cage, like soft fruit.
- **Sticky distorted leaves** Can be caused by aphids and whitefly. Spray the plants with a solution of water and liquid soap.
- **Distorted roots and poor growth** Likely to be clubroot. Pull and burn the plants, and plant brassicas elsewhere.

Cabbages

Cabbages are wonderfully easy to grow. Dark green in spring, football-sized in summer, crinkly or smooth, red or white, and variously served steamed, stuffed, pickled, raw, stir-fried or braised, you can enjoy the delights of cabbage all year round.

Spring cabbage — SOW (Aug), PLANT (Sep/Oct), HARVEST (Apr–May)

Jan	Feb	Mar	Apr	May	Jun	Jul	Aug	Sep	Oct	Nov	Dec	Jan	Feb	Mar	Apr	May	Jun	Jul	Aug	Sep	Oct	Nov	Dec

Summer cabbage — SOW (Mar), PLANT (May), HARVEST (Aug/Sep)

Jan	Feb	Mar	Apr	May	Jun	Jul	Aug	Sep	Oct	Nov	Dec	Jan	Feb	Mar	Apr	May	Jun	Jul	Aug	Sep	Oct	Nov	Dec

Winter cabbage — SOW (Apr/May), PLANT (Jun/Jul), (Depends on variety) HARVEST (Jan/Feb)

Jan	Feb	Mar	Apr	May	Jun	Jul	Aug	Sep	Oct	Nov	Dec	Jan	Feb	Mar	Apr	May	Jun	Jul	Aug	Sep	Oct	Nov	Dec

F1 Tundra

Described as 'one of the best introductions in years', this is a swift-growing winter-harvesting variety that is very frost-hardy. It can be cropped from November to April. It is a little like the Savoy, with crinkly leaves and a large, round, solid shape.

Spring Hero F1

A spring-harvesting variety that produces a huge, solid, medium green head with a white heart at the centre. Sow in August to eat in spring. It has a distinctive, sweet flavour.

Pointed Durham Early

A spring-harvesting, pointed-head variety with a good, distinctive flavour. It can be cut before the plant reaches maturity and used as spring greens.

More varieties

- **Greyhound:** A compact, summer- and autumn-harvesting variety that is a good choice for a small plot.

- **January King:** A very hardy variety that crops from December to January. The Savoy-like leaves are firm-textured and sweet-tasting.

- **Offenham:** A spring-harvesting, pointed-head variety with good texture and flavour. It can be cut early and used as spring greens.

- **Red Drumhead:** A purple-red cabbage that can be harvested from September. It has a solid, round head, perfect for pickled red cabbage.

SOIL AND SITE NEEDS

Cabbages can be grown almost anywhere, but do best on a rich, well-manured, deeply worked, firm, well-drained, moist, fertile loam on a sheltered, wind-free site. The rule is the more manure the better, but it must never be fresh or rank. The soil must be firm and compact. If it is too open, the plants will wobble at the base, resulting in loose-hearted cabbages that are subject to rots and likely to bolt. Varieties such as red cabbage require much the same conditions, the only difference being that the ground needs to be richer and more deeply worked.

SOWING AND PLANTING PROCEDURES

- Sow seeds of spring varieties in July–August, summer varieties in mid-February–early May, and winter varieties end of March–mid-May, in a prepared seed bed or in seed-trays.
- Plant out spring varieties in September–October, summer varieties in mid-April–end June, and winter varieties in mid-June–end July.
- Dib holes 30–35 cm (12–14 in) apart (10 cm/4 in for spring cabbages), with 30–35 cm (12–14 in) between rows. 'Puddle' the seedlings into the holes. Compact the soil around the plants.

SOWING AND PLANTING PROCEDURES (CONTINUED)

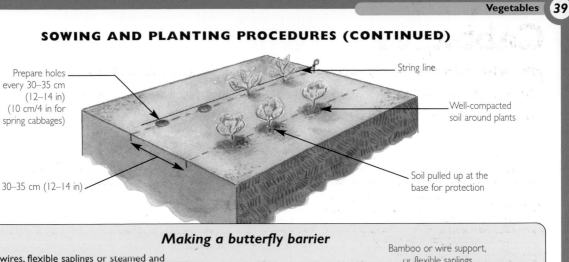

Prepare holes every 30–35 cm (12–14 in) (10 cm/4 in for spring cabbages)

String line

Well-compacted soil around plants

30–35 cm (12–14 in)

Soil pulled up at the base for protection

Making a butterfly barrier

Use stout wires, flexible saplings or steamed and bent bamboo canes to create an arched support structure over the line of cabbages. Cover the arched support with a sheet of very fine-mesh netting or fine fleece (not plastic). Hold the netting or fleece in place with bricks and rope. Tie up the ends and peg them to the ground.

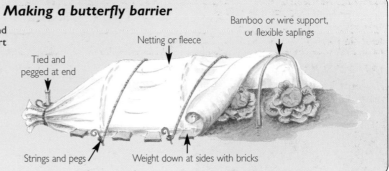

Bamboo or wire support, or flexible saplings

Netting or fleece

Tied and pegged at end

Strings and pegs

Weight down at sides with bricks

PLANT CARE

Water the young plants daily. Use the hoe to pull the soil up around the plants to give them protection against frost and wind. Be careful not to damage the fragile stems with the hoe. Once a week in dry weather, stir the surface of the soil with a hoe to create a loose-soil mulch and to keep it clean.

In extra-dry conditions, spread a deep mulch of spent manure or straw over the loose soil to hold in the residual moisture. Some growers protect against butterflies and birds by covering the plants with fleece (see above), or by growing them in a netted cage, like soft fruit.

TROUBLESHOOTING

← **Root fly** *Avoid the problem of rotting stumps and blotchy foliage by placing a felt-plastic-carpet collar around the plant to keep the egg-laying flies at bay.*

↙ **Leaf spot** *Can seriously stunt the growth of the plant. At the first signs of a problem, carefully remove and burn damaged leaves. Burn the plants at the end of the season, and the following year grow them on a different plot.*

↙ **Mealy aphids** *Shows as lumpy-looking, blue-grey colonies of aphids on the underside of leaves. Spray with a water and liquid soap solution. Burn the plants at the end of the season.*

- **Holes in leaves** *Caused by caterpillars and birds. Avoid the problem by growing the sprouts in a netted cage, like soft fruit.*
- **Distorted roots and poor growth** *Probably clubroot. Pull and burn the plants, and rotate crops in the following year.*
- **Rotting leaves** *A smelly, grey-brown rot caused by frost. Pull and burn affected plants and protect from frost next time.*

HARVESTING

You can harvest from January to March for winter cabbages, February to June for spring cabbages, and July to October for summer cabbages – the precise time depends on your chosen varieties and your growing methods. For example, if you protect the crop at both ends, then you will be able to extend the crop by harvesting as early as possible, and then leave the crop in the ground as late as possible. Use a knife to cut the cabbage off close to ground level and slash a deep X on the stump to encourage a crop of secondary mini-cabbages. Cabbage varieties such as red and white can be cut in November and December and stored in a dry, frost-free shed.

Capsicums (sweet peppers)

Grown in much the same way as tomatoes and aubergines, capsicums are, like aubergines, cultivated as much for their colour and form as for their taste. If you like salads and stir-fries, then capsicums are a very good choice for your allotment.

SOW	PLANT		HARVEST																				
Jan	Feb	Mar	Apr	May	Jun	Jul	Aug	Sep	Oct	Nov	Dec	Jan	Feb	Mar	Apr	May	Jun	Jul	Aug	Sep	Oct	Nov	Dec

F1 Beauty Bell

A sweet variety that produces an abundance of large, chunky, squarish fruits. The thick-walled peppers can be picked when they are green or left on the plant until they turn bright red.

More varieties

- **D'Asti Giallo:** A medium-early variety that has brilliant yellow, thick-fleshed fruits with a sweet, mild flavour.

- **F1 Arianne:** A sweet variety that produces light green fruits that mature to a beautiful, rich red-orange. The flesh is crisp and sweet.

- **Long Red Marconi:** A very productive variety. The long, tapered fruits turn from green to red, and the flesh is crisp and succulent.

- **Marconi Rossa:** A sweet variety with long, thin pods that are mild and sweet.

- **Sweet Spanish Mixed:** Sold as a selection of varieties to give a mix of colours and shapes. It has good, solid, squarish fruits with a mild flavour.

SOIL AND SITE NEEDS

Capsicums do best on well-drained, well-manured soil in a sunny, sheltered position. The best method is to load the manure on during the winter – the more, the merrier – and to dig it in deeply. With regard to siting, a good option is a raised bed with a plastic-screen windbreak all around; failing that, you could plant them in growing-bags in a small greenhouse, or in a pot with some sort of dedicated glass or plastic shelter. Traditionally, they were grown in a sunny border up against a wall or fence. You could maybe replicate these conditions by growing them on the sunny side of your shed.

SOWING AND PLANTING PROCEDURES

- Late February–March – sow the seeds in trays on a bed of moistened potting compost, and protect with a sheet of glass topped with newspaper. Keep warm.
- Late April–mid-May – prick the seedlings out into 7.5 cm (3 in) peat pots. Water and keep warm.
- About mid-June, when the plants are strong enough, place the peat pots in 23 cm (9 in) pots, and protect with the cloche or plastic shelter of your choice.

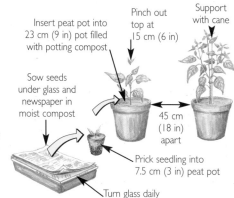

Insert peat pot into 23 cm (9 in) pot filled with potting compost

Pinch out top at 15 cm (6 in)

Support with cane

Sow seeds under glass and newspaper in moist compost

45 cm (18 in) apart

Prick seedling into 7.5 cm (3 in) peat pot

Turn glass daily

PLANT CARE

Water the seedlings before and after planting, and then water daily. Stir the surface of the soil with a hoe or trowel to create a loose-soil mulch and to keep it clean. Support the plants with a cane and ties, and pinch out the tip when the plant reaches 15 cm (6 in) in height. You could spread a mulch of spent manure or straw over the loose soil to hold in the moisture.

HARVESTING

You can harvest from July to October – the date depends on the variety, and whether you want to pick the peppers when they are green or wait until they ripen to red. Use a sharp knife to cut the fruits as needed.

TROUBLESHOOTING

- **Rolled leaves** Caused by low temperatures. Protect the plants with some kind of screen or cover.
- **Mouldy fruits and leaves** Caused by virus diseases that attack in wet and cold conditions. Symptoms include mouldy leaves and fruits, spotted stems and general damage to the flesh of the fruit. Remove all affected fruits and leaves, as well as litter on the ground around the plant. Wash the plant with a solution of water and liquid soap.

Carrots

Everyone knows about carrots. They look good, they smell good, they taste good, they do you good, they are relatively easy to grow, most children like them, there are lots of varieties and, best of all, they can be eaten right through from early June to Christmas.

SOW				HARVEST																			
Jan	Feb	Mar	Apr	May	Jun	Jul	Aug	Sep	Oct	Nov	Dec	Jan	Feb	Mar	Apr	May	Jun	Jul	Aug	Sep	Oct	Nov	Dec

F1 Flyaway

This is the first fly-resistant variety. It is not the complete answer to the dreaded carrot fly, but it is a step in the right direction. It produces large, stumpy, smooth-skinned carrots with good colour and texture, and a fine flavour.

More varieties

- **Chantenay Red Cored:** An old mid-season or maincrop variety. It produces stump-ended roots with good colour, taste and texture.

- **Early Market:** A late- and early-season variety with short, fat, stumpy roots, suitable for good, shallow soil.

- **Early Nantes:** A reliable mid-season variety good for successive sowing, with long, tasty, blunt-ended roots.

- **James Scarlet Intermediate:** A maincrop variety with very tasty, long, broad-shouldered, deep orange roots.

- **Topscore:** A Nantes variety that produces long, dark orange roots, 18–20 cm (7–8 in) long, of a uniform shape, with good texture and taste.

SOIL AND SITE NEEDS

While you can grow carrots on just about any well-cultivated allotment soil, they do best on a friable, deeply dug, well-drained, sandy, fertile loam in a sunny position. If your soil is a nice, crumbly, sandy loam, you can grow the long-rooted types; otherwise, if it is a bit hard and heavier, then it is best to grow the short, stumpy varieties that thrive in such conditions. Be warned: if your soil is overly stony or contains great lumps of fresh manure, the likelihood is that the growing root will divide, resulting in a carrot that is stunted or forked.

SOWING AND PLANTING PROCEDURES

- Early March–late June (depending upon variety) – create 18 mm (¾ in) deep drills 15–23 cm (6–9 in) apart. Sow seeds thinly, compact the soil, and water with a fine sprinkler.
- Thin the seedlings so they are about 5 cm (2 in) apart.
- Use cloches – glass, corrugated plastic or a plastic polytunnel – to protect the plants at the beginning and end of the season.

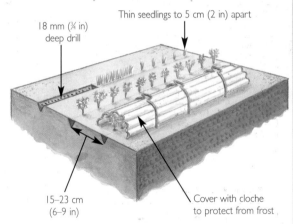

18 mm (¾ in) deep drill

Thin seedlings to 5 cm (2 in) apart

15–23 cm (6–9 in)

Cover with cloche to protect from frost

PLANT CARE

Keep the plants free from weeds and the soil in a loose condition by frequent hoeing. This loose-soil mulch helps to retain the moisture in the soil below by ensuring steady growth, which in turn prevents the roots from splitting.

HARVESTING

You can harvest from May to December, if you have made successive sowings of a range of varieties, and if you protect the crops so that they can stay in the ground. Store maincrop carrots in boxes of sand in a frost-free shed.

TROUBLESHOOTING

- **Rust-coloured tunnels** Tunnels and rots caused by the carrot fly. Avoid the problem by growing onions alongside the carrots.
- **Splitting** Caused by wet-dry-wet conditions. Avoid the problem by spreading a mulch of spent manure to retain residual moisture.
- **Green top** Caused by the top of the carrot being exposed. Avoid the problem by hoeing up the soil.

Cauliflowers

Growing cauliflowers can be a challenge, but cooking them is easy. You can use cauliflower in soups or sauces, but in my opinion the best method is to steam it for about eight minutes and then serve it up with bread and butter, and Stilton cheese.

SOW	PLANT			HARVEST About nine months of the year depending on variety

Jan	Feb	Mar	Apr	May	Jun	Jul	Aug	Sep	Oct	Nov	Dec	Jan	Feb	Mar	Apr	May	Jun	Jul	Aug	Sep	Oct	Nov	Dec

Dominant

A good variety for summer and autumn harvesting. It produces large, compact, slightly creamy-coloured heads, and can be cropped from July onwards. It is a good option for a dry, windy plot.

More varieties

- **Autumn Giant:** A good, old, reliable, summer- and autumn-harvesting variety that has been around for at least 100 years. It produces large, solid, white heads, and will do its best against all odds.

- **Leamington:** A good, old-fashioned, winter- and spring-harvesting variety that produces large, solid, slightly less than uniform heads.

- **Snowball:** An old, dwarf, summer- and autumn-harvesting variety that produces small, tight heads that can be cut from June to September.

- **White Rock:** A good variety for harvesting from August onwards. It produces beautiful, tight, white heads, well hidden in a shell of leaves.

SOIL AND SITE NEEDS

Cauliflowers need a deep, well-manured, compact, well-drained, moisture-retentive soil in a sunny location. The manure or organic matter should not be fresh, rank or sitting on the surface. The ideal is to manure for some other crop, and then follow on with cauliflowers. If the soil is really poor and or dry, or in any way grossly undernourished, give up the idea of cauliflowers and grow another crop. Put another way, the plants will grow in poor conditions, but the heads will come to nothing and you will be disappointed.

SOWING AND PLANTING PROCEDURES

- Mid-March–late May – sow seeds in a prepared seed bed or seed-trays.
- June–July – plant out on a dull, rainy day, so that you do not have to water.
- Dib holes 50–60 cm (20–24 in) apart, with 50–60 cm (20–24 in) between rows. Use water to 'puddle' the seedlings into the holes.
- Use your fingers to compact the soil around the plants, and water generously.
- Fit loose-fit plastic/felt collars to protect the plants from root fly.

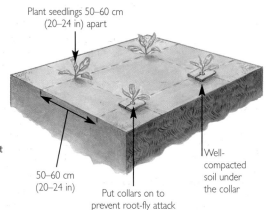

Plant seedlings 50–60 cm (20–24 in) apart

50–60 cm (20–24 in)

Put collars on to prevent root-fly attack

Well-compacted soil under the collar

PLANT CARE

Water the seedlings before and after planting. Stir the surface of the soil with a hoe to create a loose-soil mulch and to keep it clean, and spread a mulch of chopped straw to hold in the moisture. Water copiously. As soon as a head shows, break a leaf over it in order to keep it clean.

HARVESTING

If you sow early, autumn and winter varieties and provide shelter, you can harvest for 9–10 months of the year. Cut complete with the wraparound leaves, or lift the whole plant and store in a frost-free shed.

TROUBLESHOOTING

- **Leaf spot** Shows as rusty spots on the leaves. Burn the plants at the end of the season. Rotate the crops.
- **Mealy aphid** Shows as blue-grey aphids on the underside of leaves. Spray with a water and liquid soap solution. Burn the plants at the end of the season.
- **Holes in leaves** Caused by caterpillars and birds. Avoid the problem by growing in a netted cage.

Celeriac

Celeriac is a winner on many counts. It has a certain rarity value, it is good fun to grow, it looks impressive once it has grown, it is delicious as a winter soup, and it is perfect in a winter salad. It will also serve to impress your neighbouring allotment-holders.

	SOW		PLANT								HARVEST												
Jan	Feb	Mar	Apr	May	Jun	Jul	Aug	Sep	Oct	Nov	Dec	Jan	Feb	Mar	Apr	May	Jun	Jul	Aug	Sep	Oct	Nov	Dec

Balder

A popular variety, grown as a half-hardy annual, that produces large, round, brown roots with lots of dark green foliage. The white, crisp-textured flesh has a good celery flavour. It is very tasty boiled and mashed, as with a turnip, but even better grated into a winter salad.

More varieties

- **Giant Prague:** A good, reliable variety that produces large, brilliant green-yellow, ball-like roots with medium-green foliage. It can be harvested from late September onwards. It has good, solid, strong-tasting flesh, and stores well.

- **Prinz:** A very popular variety that resists leaf disease and bolting. It has a thin, light skin, crisp, white flesh, and a characteristic scented flavour. It makes a really good picnic meal – try grated celeriac, sliced onion rings and a wedge of strong cheddar cheese between two thick slices of fresh brown bread.

SOIL AND SITE NEEDS

Celeriac or turnip-rooted celery is much easier to grow than celery, in that it is grown on the flat, and it does not need to be blanched. It likes a well-manured soil, with the manure having been dug in the preceding winter, on an open, sunny but sheltered site where it can enjoy a long, uninterrupted growing season. When the root is swelling, you must make sure that the soil is kept moist – provide as much water as possible in dry spells. Be warned that the young plants do not like cold winds, and the roots will stop swelling if you miss out on the watering.

SOWING AND PLANTING PROCEDURES

- March–April – sow seeds under glass in prepared seed-trays.
- Pot the seedlings on, as soon as they are big enough to handle, into peat pots or trays at a spacing of 5 cm (2 in).
- May–June – plant out 30 cm (1 ft) apart, with 25–38 cm (10–15 in) between rows. Set the plants as 'shallow' as possible, so that they are sitting on rather than in the holes.
- Trim off the sideshoots after planting.

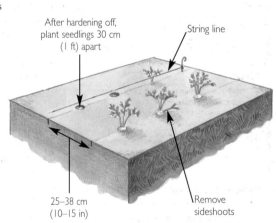

After hardening off, plant seedlings 30 cm (1 ft) apart

String line

25–38 cm (10–15 in)

Remove sideshoots

PLANT CARE

Water the plants daily. Stir the surface of the soil with a hoe to create a loose-soil mulch and to keep it clean. Remove old leaves, and any wandering shoots and roots, as soon as the need arises. Never allow the ground to dry out. Keep hoeing to keep the ground free from weeds and bugs.

HARVESTING

If your site is well drained, and you protect the plants with straw and fleece, you can leave the crop in the ground, and harvest from November to March. If your soil is wet, lift and store in a frost-free shed.

TROUBLESHOOTING

- **Rust-coloured tunnels** Tunnels and rots caused by the carrot fly. Avoid the problem by growing onions alongside the celeriac.
- **Splitting** Caused by drought/flood conditions. Avoid the problem by spreading a mulch of spent manure to retain residual moisture.
- **Slugs** Cause damage to young leaves. Gather the slugs by hand.

Celery

Growing celery is undoubtedly a sweat-making challenge – digging trenches, earthing up the plants, regular watering, more earthing up, and so on – but the experience of eating freshly picked celery with bread and cheese makes it all worthwhile.

| SOW | PLANT | | HARVEST | | | | | | | | | | | | | | | | | | | |
| Jan | Feb | Mar | Apr | May | Jun | Jul | Aug | Sep | Oct | Nov | Dec | Jan | Feb | Mar | Apr | May | Jun | Jul | Aug | Sep | Oct | Nov | Dec |

Pascal

A good, reliable trench variety that produces huge, solid heads of crisp, white to green stalks. From a cook's viewpoint, it is a good all-rounder – try it in a Waldorf salad, in a chunk as a starter, with bread and cheese, in a soup, braised – it is tender, crisp and tasty.

More varieties

- **Giant Red:** A hardy variety with a slightly loose and open form. It has very solid, dark red-purple heads that blanch down to pink-white. It is ready right through the Christmas period.

- **Giant White:** A popular white variety, much like Giant Red.

- **Golden Self-blanching:** A good, dwarf variety for growers who want to avoid blanching. The flavour is undoubtedly much blander than that of most traditional varieties, but it is much easier to grow.

- **Green Utah:** A self-blanching variety that is very popular in America. It produces large heads with green stalks. It has a crisp texture and characteristic flavour.

SOIL AND SITE NEEDS

Being semi-aquatic, celery does best in a deep, rich, heavy, moist but well-drained soil, in a position that is open and sunny. It is worth noting that the phrase 'moist but well-drained' means that the soil needs to be damp, even wet, but not so wet that the water 'puddles' or remains on the surface. Celery needs lots of moisture, but will not thrive if the soil is waterlogged or sour. Make sure that the ground is prepared with well-rotted manure. The piled earth (the earth that you have drawn to the side in preparation for earthing up) must be repeatedly worked so that it is fine and friable.

SOWING AND PLANTING PROCEDURES

- March–April – sow seeds under glass in prepared seed-trays.
- Pot the seedlings on, as soon as they are big enough to handle, into peat pots or trays at a spacing of 5 cm (2 in).
- May to June – dig a trench 30 cm (1 ft) deep and 55 cm (22 in) wide. Put manure topped up with earth into the trench, to within 7.5 cm (3 in) of the surface, and set the plants 23 cm (9 in) apart in the trench; for self-blanching varieties, increase this to 27 cm (11 in).

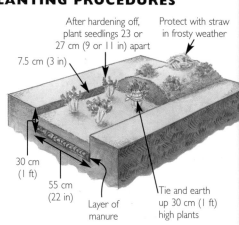

After hardening off, plant seedlings 23 or 27 cm (9 or 11 in) apart

Protect with straw in frosty weather

7.5 cm (3 in)

30 cm (1 ft)

55 cm (22 in)

Layer of manure

Tie and earth up 30 cm (1 ft) high plants

PLANT CARE

Water the plants daily. Stir the surface of the soil with a hoe to create a loose-soil mulch. Remove suckers and dead leaves. When the plants are about 25–30 cm (10–12 in) high, bind them with raffia, and then repeatedly earth up so as to create a ridge or mound that covers all but the foliage. Cover with chopped straw in frosty weather.

HARVESTING

You can harvest self-blanching varieties from August to early November, and traditional varieties from November to March. Use a fork to ease the plant from the ground. Leave remaining plants covered.

TROUBLESHOOTING

- **Brown spotted leaves** Caused by any number of viruses and fungi. Pull and burn the plants and change to a different variety.
- **Slugs and snails** Can cause secondary damage. Gather the pests on a daily basis.
- **Brown rot** Shows itself as a rotten heart at the lifting stage. Burn the plants and try again on another plot.

Chicory

If you enjoy crisp, strong, tart flavours in your winter salads, and you have a greenhouse or cold frame, and the use of a shed, and you do not mind waiting a good part of the year before you get a crop, then chicory is a relatively easy-to-grow option.

| | | | | | SOW | | | | | | | HARVEST | | | | | | | | | | | |
| Jan | Feb | Mar | Apr | May | Jun | Jul | Aug | Sep | Oct | Nov | Dec | Jan | Feb | Mar | Apr | May | Jun | Jul | Aug | Sep | Oct | Nov | Dec |

Brussels Witloof
A popular, reliable, easy-to-grow variety that has good-sized, carrot-like roots. After blanching, the roots produce medium-sized, yellow-white chicons. The chicons are crisp, succulent and characteristically mildly bitter and tasty – perfect in sandwiches or a salad.

More varieties

- **F1 Zoom:** An easy-to-blanch variety that produces good-sized, carrot-like roots from September onwards. Although the chicons are undoubtedly crisp and tasty, some aficionados feel that the taste is a bit lacking.

- **Red (Radicchio) Late Rossa di Chioggia:** A frost-resistant variety that produces huge, succulent, red-white chicons. This is a good choice for an exposed plot that is subject to frosts.

- **Red (Radicchio) Variegata di Chioggia:** A variety extensively grown in Italy that produces large multi-coloured, ball-like chicons, like large rosettes. Many people consider this variety to be the very best.

SOIL AND SITE NEEDS

The soil needs to be light to medium, soft in texture, deeply dug (the deeper the better), fertile and moist. Avoid freshly manured ground, because the roots of the growing chicory will hit the fresh manure and divide. The best method is to spread the manure for one crop, and then follow on with chicory. To test the soil, take a handful and roll it in your hands in order to feel the texture. It should feel friable, meaning crumbly with no hard bits or sticky lumps. Choose a sunny corner, well away from draughts.

SOWING AND PLANTING PROCEDURES

- Early May–mid-July – create 12 mm (½ in) deep drills 25–30 cm (10–12 in) apart; sow seeds thinly, compact the soil, and water with a fine sprinkler.
- Thin the seedlings until they are 20 cm (8 in) apart.

PLANT CARE

Water daily. Stir the surface of the soil with a hoe to create a loose-soil mulch. When the leaves have died down, lift and trim the roots to remove forked roots and earth, and bed them down flat in dry sand.

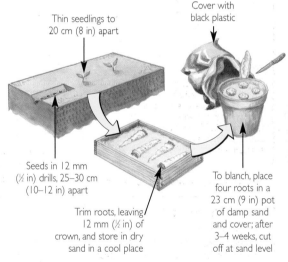

Thin seedlings to 20 cm (8 in) apart

Cover with black plastic

Seeds in 12 mm (½ in) drills, 25–30 cm (10–12 in) apart

Trim roots, leaving 12 mm (½ in) of crown, and store in dry sand in a cool place

To blanch, place four roots in a 23 cm (9 in) pot of damp sand and cover; after 3–4 weeks, cut off at sand level

HARVESTING

You can harvest and eat self-blanching varieties from October to December. You can blanch traditional types from mid-November to April. Take four roots at a time (ones that you stored in October and November), set them in damp sand in a 23 cm (9 in) pot and cover with black plastic. They will be ready in 3–4 weeks. Cut them off just above sand level.

TROUBLESHOOTING

- **Slugs** Pick the pests off by hand.
- **Leaf and stem damage** Evidence of cutworms. Hoe the ground around the plants and physically search out the fat, creamy-brown caterpillars.
- **Heart rot** Shows as yellowy-brown damage to the leaves. Can be caused either by frost damage or by a virus. Avoid the problem by using frost- and virus-resistant varieties.

Cucumbers

If you enjoy growing tomatoes and capsicums (sweet peppers), then you will probably like growing cucumbers too. They are perfect in salads and sandwiches, and some varieties are also good for pickling. You have the choice of growing cucumbers under cloches or outside.

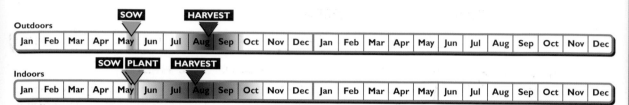

Outdoors — SOW (May), HARVEST (Aug)

| Jan | Feb | Mar | Apr | May | Jun | Jul | Aug | Sep | Oct | Nov | Dec | Jan | Feb | Mar | Apr | May | Jun | Jul | Aug | Sep | Oct | Nov | Dec |

Indoors — SOW PLANT (May), HARVEST (Aug)

| Jan | Feb | Mar | Apr | May | Jun | Jul | Aug | Sep | Oct | Nov | Dec | Jan | Feb | Mar | Apr | May | Jun | Jul | Aug | Sep | Oct | Nov | Dec |

Telegraph Improved

An improved traditional variety that can be grown outside, in a cloche, or in a cold frame. It produces a good straight fruit, similar to that of Rollinsons Telegraph, a variety that was grown at the beginning of the twentieth century.

More varieties

- **Bedfordshire Prize:** An outdoor variety that produces an abundance of short, slightly ridged fruits, firm and crisp with a slightly bitter taste.

- **F1 Prolific:** An early-fruiting, disease-resistant outdoor variety with short to medium fruits. It likes support, and you can grow it outside in mild areas.

- **Gherkin:** A swift-growing outdoor variety, suitable for pickling, with short, stubby, slightly prickly fruits.

- **King George:** An indoor variety that produces long, straight, dark green fruits that are crisp and tasty.

SOIL AND SITE NEEDS

The soil needs to be light to medium, soft in texture, deeply dug, well-manured and moist. The best method is to dig pits or a trench within the plot, and then top the pits/trenches up with a mix of compost and/or well-rotted manure. Choose a spot in full sun, away from draughts, and put a plastic screen or shelter on the windward side.

SOWING AND PLANTING PROCEDURES

- Indoor varieties – in mid- to late May, sow the seeds in trays on moistened tissue and cover with newspaper. Keep warm.
- Late May – prick the seedlings into 7.5 cm (3 in) peat pots and later into 23 cm (9 in) pots or growing-bags. Cover with glass or plastic.
- Outdoor varieties – in mid- to late May, dig trenches 30 cm (1 ft) deep and 30 cm (1 ft) wide, and fill with manure and soil. Sow groups of three seeds 18 mm (¾ in) deep, at 60–90 cm (2–3 ft) intervals, and cover with plastic bottles.
- Thin each group of three to the best plant and protect the base with a mulch.

Indoor varieties

Cover with newspaper

Seeds on moistened tissue

7.5 cm (3 in) peat pot

23 cm (9 in) pot of potting compost

Outdoor varieties

Three seeds 18 mm (¾ in) deep, covered with a plastic bottle

Thin seedlings to one plant and mulch around base

30 cm (1 ft) deep and wide

Manure

PLANT CARE

Support indoor plants with canes and ties. Pinch out the growing tip when it reaches the top of your greenhouse or cloche. Let outdoor plants trail along the ground. Stop the side-growing shoots when they get to your frame or boundary. Water daily.

HARVESTING

Harvest indoor varieties from June to October, and outdoor varieties from end July to end September. Support the fruits and cut them off with a sharp knife.

TROUBLESHOOTING

- **Withered fruits** Could be root rot or some other root problem caused by drought. Remove the damaged fruits, and water daily.
- **Slugs and snails** Show as damaged trails and pits to the fruits. Gather the pests by hand.
- **Bitter fruits** Caused by drought/wet/cold conditions. Water daily and surround the plant with a plastic screen.

Endives

The great thing about endives is that they can be harvested from late August to April – just the thing to lift the gloom of winter. If you get it right, you can be eating lettuces in the spring and summer, and then follow on straight away with endives.

| SOW | | | | | HARVEST | | | | | | | | | | | | | | | | | | |
|Jan|Feb|Mar|Apr|May|Jun|Jul|Aug|Sep|Oct|Nov|Dec|Jan|Feb|Mar|Apr|May|Jun|Jul|Aug|Sep|Oct|Nov|Dec|

Pancalieri
A popular variety that produces huge heads with lots of dark green, lace-edged leaves. Although it can be blanched, just like other varieties, the head is so huge and dense that the heart is in effect self-blanching.

More varieties

- **Moss Curled:** A tried-and-trusted, traditional, easy-to-grow variety that has been popular at least since the beginning of the twentieth century. It is a good choice for growing in a protected corner. Endive aficionados say that the texture and taste of Moss Curled cannot be beaten.

- **Scarola Verde:** A very popular, swift-blanching variety for spring and summer use. It produces very large, frilly-edged, green-white heads. It can be blanched in 2–3 days.

- **Wallone:** A self-blanching French type that is good for growing in a polytunnel. It produces a large, densely packed head that results in a self-blanching heart. It can be cropped from November to January.

SOIL AND SITE NEEDS

Endives do best in a deeply dug, rich but not too heavy, fertile soil that contains plenty of well-rotted manure from a previous crop. A good method is to prepare a bed that is raised up above the overall level, so that you can control the soil mix and ensure good drainage. You need a sunny, open spot for summer and autumn varieties, and partial shade for spring ones. Be aware that spring-grown endives have a tendency to bolt if they get too much sun. The best all-round solution is to choose a sunny, open position in the knowledge that you will have to use screens to provide shade.

SOWING AND PLANTING PROCEDURES

- Mid-March–early September – create 12 mm (½ in) deep drills 25–30 cm (10–12 in) apart. Sow seeds thinly, compact the soil and water generously.
- Thin the seedlings to 30 cm (1 ft) apart.
- Water generously throughout, especially if the weather is dry, but never allow the plants to sit in a puddle of water.

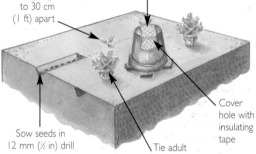

Thin seedlings to 30 cm (1 ft) apart

Blanch by covering for 2–3 weeks with a pot raised up to allow for ventilation

Cover hole with insulating tape

Sow seeds in 12 mm (½ in) drill

Tie adult plant loosely

PLANT CARE

Water daily. Stir the surface of the soil with a hoe to create a loose-soil mulch. Endives must be blanched, or they are useless. Blanch the plants sometime between July and October, when they are fully grown. Choose a warm, sunny day when the air is dry, and then gently gather the leaves together, bind them up with raffia, and cover with a clay flower pot.

HARVESTING

You can harvest about 2–3 weeks after covering the plant with the flower pot. Check the plant every day or so to make sure it is dry and free from slugs. Sometime after the second week, lift the pot and use a knife to cut the plant off close to the ground.

TROUBLESHOOTING

- **Bolting** Caused by wet/drought conditions. Avoid the problem by regular, little-and-often watering.
- **Slugs and snails** Gather by hand.
- **Brown rot** Shows as damage to the heart after the plant has been blanched. Usually caused by slugs and/or poor blanching techniques – by having the binding too tight, or covering the plant when it is wet.

Kale

Kale, also known as borecole and curly kale, grows just about anywhere, it is hardy, and it can be harvested from November to early April. The young leaves and shoots are delicious when lightly steamed and served with meat or fish, or covered with a cheese sauce.

SOW		**PLANT**							**HARVEST**														
Jan	Feb	Mar	Apr	May	Jun	Jul	Aug	Sep	Oct	Nov	Dec	Jan	Feb	Mar	Apr	May	Jun	Jul	Aug	Sep	Oct	Nov	Dec

Dwarf Green Curled

A very popular, hardy, old variety that produces a mass of densely curled, dark green leaves on a central stalk. It is a good choice for difficult plots, as it seems to do better in frosty weather.

More varieties

- **Cottagers:** A traditional, very hardy variety that produces lots of medium green leaves with a good texture and a strong, distinctive flavour. Discard all but the young, tender leaves.

- **Nero di Toscana:** A traditional Italian variety, sometimes sold as Black Russian. It has dark green, bubbled, tongue-like leaves on a short stem.

- **Red Russian:** A large variety that produces lots of crinkly green-purple leaves on a tall stem. Food buffs say that the colour, texture and taste improve after a frost.

- **Westland Winter:** A very hardy variety. It produces masses of curled blue-green leaves. This is a really good choice for a difficult, exposed plot.

SOIL AND SITE NEEDS

Kale does well on almost any soil but, like all brassicas, does really well on a strong, deeply worked, well-compacted, fertile loam. The soil needs plenty of manure, but there must not be so much that the plants grow rapidly and become soft. As with many other crops, a good method is to spread the manure for one crop, hoe the surface of the soil just enough to remove the weeds, and then follow on with the kale. The plants will thereby start off slowly and become hardy. Choose a sunny corner. Be mindful that kale will put up with just about anything, apart from loose ground, standing water and a long, hard, bitter frost.

SOWING AND PLANTING PROCEDURES

- Mid-April–end of May – sow seeds in a prepared seed bed or in seed-trays.
- Mid-June–early August – planting out is best done on a dull, rainy day so that you do not have to water.
- Dib holes 38–45 cm (15–18 in) apart, with 45–50 cm (18–20 in) between rows. 'Puddle' the seedlings into the holes and use your fingers to compact the soil around the plants. Water frequently over the next few days.

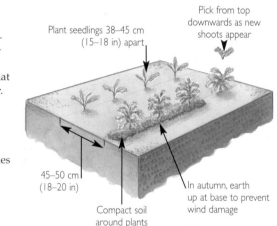

Plant seedlings 38–45 cm (15–18 in) apart

Pick from top downwards as new shoots appear

45–50 cm (18–20 in)

Compact soil around plants

In autumn, earth up at base to prevent wind damage

PLANT CARE

Water daily. Stir the surface of the soil with a hoe to create a loose-soil mulch, and draw the earth up around the plants to give support and to protect them from wind and frost. While kale will do well on an exposed plot, if it is very windy you will need to rig up some sort of screen on the windward side.

HARVESTING

You can harvest from November to May. Use a knife to nip out the crown, and then work down the plant picking off the sideshoots. Throw away all the old and yellow leaves.

TROUBLESHOOTING

- **Mealy aphid** Shows as lumpy-looking, blue-grey colonies of aphids on the underside of leaves. Spray with a water and liquid soap solution. Burn the plants at the end of the season.
- **Poor growth and yellow leaves** Probably caused by wind rock. Stake the plants and grow dwarf varieties next time.

Kohl rabi

The good thing about kohl rabi is that it can be sitting on your plate 6–8 weeks after sowing. As for the taste, once you know that *Kohlrabi* is German for 'cabbage turnip', then you just about know it all. It is delicious when steamed and mashed with butter.

SOW — Jun | HARVEST — Sep

| Jan | Feb | Mar | Apr | May | Jun | Jul | Aug | Sep | Oct | Nov | Dec | Jan | Feb | Mar | Apr | May | Jun | Jul | Aug | Sep | Oct | Nov | Dec |

F1 White Danube

A very popular, late variety that produces a white-fleshed, green-skinned root. The taste and texture have been compared to Green Delicacy.

More varieties

- **Green Delicacy:** An early variety that has a fist-sized root with a pale green skin and white flesh. The fine textured flesh has a slightly milder flavour than Purple Delicacy. It grows to about 200 g (7 oz) in weight.

- **Logo:** A variety resistant to bolting and splitting that has smallish, flat, round roots with tender, tasty flesh.

- **Purple Delicacy:** A late variety that produces a root with a purple skin and white flesh. This variety is later and hardier than Green Delicacy. The flesh is tender with a strong flavour.

- **Superschmelz:** A large, slow-to-bolt variety that produces, it is claimed, roots up to 8 kg (18 lb) in weight, but what would you do with them?

SOIL AND SITE NEEDS

Kohl rabi likes a light to medium, soft-textured, moist, fertile soil, much like turnips. In fact, it needs everything that a turnip needs, the only difference being that, as the kohl rabi sits on rather than in the ground, the soil does not need to be worked to any great depth. It needs a sheltered, warm spot, but not overly sunny, and plenty of water. Be warned that, if you are a bit tardy with the water, the plant may come to a halt and bolt without plumping up.

SOWING AND PLANTING PROCEDURES

- Mid-March–August (depending upon variety) – create 18 mm (¾ in) deep drills 25–30 cm (10–12 in) apart. Sow a pinch of seeds every 13–15 cm (5–6 in). Compact the soil and use a fine spray to water generously.
- When the seedlings are big enough to handle, thin out to leave the strong plants at 15 cm (6 in) intervals.
- Water generously in dry weather – as much as you can manage.

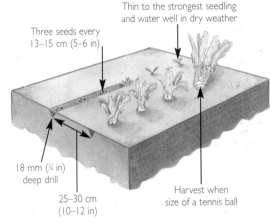

Three seeds every 13–15 cm (5–6 in)

Thin to the strongest seedling and water well in dry weather

18 mm (¾ in) deep drill

25–30 cm (10–12 in)

Harvest when size of a tennis ball

PLANT CARE

Stir the surface of the soil with a hoe to create a loose-soil mulch and water generously. If the weather is very dry, spread a mulch of spent manure or chopped straw. Remove yellow leaves. Break off sideshoot growths and any side foliage so as to keep a smooth, rounded shape.

HARVESTING

You can harvest from June to December – the precise time depends on your chosen variety. Use a fork to ease the globes out of the ground. Lift as needed. They spoil if left in the ground too long, and they spoil if stored.

TROUBLESHOOTING

- **Poor root size** Often caused by crowding and/or failure to remove all the sideshoots. Always follow the spacing advice.
- **Sticky yellow foliage** Caused by colonies of aphids on the underside of leaves. Spray with a water and liquid soap solution. Burn all affected plants at the end of the season.
- **Woody texture** Caused by allowing the plant to grow too big. It is best to pull when the plant is small and tender.

Marrows and courgettes

There is something really exciting about growing marrows and courgettes – it might be the shape or the size. One thing I know for sure is that freshly picked courgettes fried in olive oil are a treat that should not be missed. If you like growing marrows, you will like growing courgettes.

	SOW	PLANT		HARVEST																			
Jan	Feb	Mar	Apr	May	Jun	Jul	Aug	Sep	Oct	Nov	Dec	Jan	Feb	Mar	Apr	May	Jun	Jul	Aug	Sep	Oct	Nov	Dec

All Green Bush
A high-yielding courgette variety that produces masses of dark green fruits. They are very tasty if you cut them when they are about 10 cm (4 in) long and fry them in olive oil. The more you cut, the more will grow.

More varieties

- **F1 Jemmer:** A bright yellow courgette that is useful if you want to create colourful meals. You could have a barbecue with a mix of courgettes of different sizes, shapes and colours, together with peppers and tomatoes.

- **Long Green Bush:** A prolific marrow that produces large fruits – perfect if you like stuffed and roasted marrow. The fruits also store well.

- **Zucchini:** A courgette variety that produces small, dark-skinned, tight-fleshed fruits – perfect for cooking on a barbecue. Be aware that, if you let the fruits grow big, the plant will wind down and stop producing, and the large fruits will have an open texture and a watery taste.

SOIL AND SITE NEEDS

Marrows and courgettes can be grown on just about any soil, but they do best on deeply worked, well-manured, moist but well-drained soil. The key words here are 'moist but well-drained'. As with cucumbers and celery, a good method is to dig holes or trenches and build a heap of well-rotted manure and compost. Fill a hole with manure, cover it with a flat mound of manure topped with a few centimetres (inches) of earth, and then put the plants in place. The mound not only catches the sun, but it also ensures that the soil is well drained. Once the plants are hardened off and growing well, cover the mound with a mulch to hold in the moisture.

SOWING AND PLANTING PROCEDURES

- Mid-April–early May – sow 2–3 seeds in peat pots under glass or plastic. Thin the seedlings to one good plant.
- Mid-May–mid-June – dig holes 30 cm (1 ft) deep, 30 cm (1 ft) wide, in lines 1.2–1.5 m (4–5 ft) apart (90 cm/3 ft for bush varieties), and fill with well-rotted manure. Build a soil-manure mound over the hole. Set the peat-pot plants into the top of the mound and water generously.

PLANT CARE

Stir the surface of the soil with a hoe to create a loose-soil mulch. Spread a mulch of spent manure around the plant. Pinch out tips of lateral shoots at about 60 cm (2 ft). Keep watering and mulching throughout the season with grass clippings and more spent manure – it all helps to plump up the crop. Place a tray or piece of wood under the fruit.

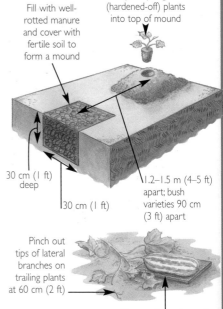

Fill with well-rotted manure and cover with fertile soil to form a mound

Transplant pot-grown (hardened-off) plants into top of mound

30 cm (1 ft) deep

30 cm (1 ft)

1.2–1.5 m (4–5 ft) apart; bush varieties 90 cm (3 ft) apart

Pinch out tips of lateral branches on trailing plants at 60 cm (2 ft)

Tray or piece of wood

HARVESTING

You can harvest from July to October. Cut courgettes as needed, preferably every few days to keep them producing. Cut marrows as needed. At the end of the season they can be hung in nets, and stored in a frost-free shed.

TROUBLESHOOTING

- **Slugs and snails** These are the biggest nuisance, especially when the plants are young and tender. Do not plant out until the stems are protected by a matt of hairs. Always be on the lookout, stirring the soil, tidying up dead leaves and gathering the pests.

Onions and shallots

During my childhood, my grandfather told me that 'the pyramids were built on onions'; he must have known of the inscription on the Great Pyramid that tells how the builders were in part paid in onions. They are now a staple part of many people's diets, and a delight to grow and eat.

From sets — **SOW** (Mar) — **HARVEST** (Aug)

Jan	Feb	Mar	Apr	May	Jun	Jul	Aug	Sep	Oct	Nov	Dec	Jan	Feb	Mar	Apr	May	Jun	Jul	Aug	Sep	Oct	Nov	Dec

Spring sowing – from seed for summer — **SOW** (Mar) — **HARVEST** (Aug)

Jan	Feb	Mar	Apr	May	Jun	Jul	Aug	Sep	Oct	Nov	Dec	Jan	Feb	Mar	Apr	May	Jun	Jul	Aug	Sep	Oct	Nov	Dec

Summer sowing – from seed to overwinter — **SOW** (Aug) — **HARVEST** (Aug)

Jan	Feb	Mar	Apr	May	Jun	Jul	Aug	Sep	Oct	Nov	Dec	Jan	Feb	Mar	Apr	May	Jun	Jul	Aug	Sep	Oct	Nov	Dec

Senshyu Yellow

An overwintering, heavy-yielding, Japanese variety that produces good-sized, spherical, white-fleshed onions. This is a good choice if you want to be sowing during late summer and cropping in the following June.

More varieties

- **Ailsa Craig:** A tried-and-trusted, old, exhibition variety producing large, golden-skinned, mild-flavoured onions.

- **Bedford Champion:** A very popular, old-fashioned variety that produces large, tasty onions that store well.

- **Golden Gourmet:** A Dutch-type shallot with small, crisp, tasty bulbs.

- **Red Brunswick:** A large, purple-red variety with huge, tasty, onions.

SOIL AND SITE NEEDS

Onions do best on a deeply worked, well-manured, moist, well-drained, friable, fertile, sandy soil in a sunny position. Ideally, the manure needs to be well broken down and rotted – dig it in during autumn so that it is ready for spring sowing. Generally, if your soil is sandy, it needs a dressing of ground clay; if it is heavy and sticky, it needs a dressing of sand or grit.

SOWING AND PLANTING PROCEDURES

- Spring sowing (February–April) – create 12 mm (½ in) deep drills, 25 cm (10 in) apart. Sow seeds thinly. Thin seedlings to 2.5–5 cm (1–2 in) apart, depending upon variety.
- Summer sowing (August–September) – create 12 mm (½ in) deep drills, 25 cm (10 in) apart. Sow seeds thinly. Thin seedlings to 5 cm (2 in) apart.
- Spring sets (February–April) – plant sets 5–7.5 cm (2–3 in) apart, in rows 25 cm (10 in) apart.
- Exhibition onions (January) – sow seeds in a tray on a windowsill. Plant out in April 7.5 cm (3 in) apart, in rows 30–38 cm (12–15 in) apart.

PLANT CARE

Stir the surface of the soil with a hoe to create a loose-soil mulch. Later use your fingers to draw the soil slightly away, so that the swelling bulb sits high on the surface. Do not water, but rather keep stirring the ground with the hoe so as to prevent the moisture wicking out from the underlying moist soil.

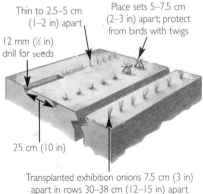

Thin to 2.5–5 cm (1–2 in) apart

Place sets 5–7.5 cm (2–3 in) apart; protect from birds with twigs

12 mm (½ in) drill for seeds

25 cm (10 in)

Transplanted exhibition onions 7.5 cm (3 in) apart in rows 30–38 cm (12–15 in) apart

HARVESTING

Harvest from June to September. Lift large and salad onions as needed. To ripen and store, bend the tops over. When the tops are yellow, lift and dry the onions in the sun. Put them in boxes, or string them up, and store in a frost-free shed.

TROUBLESHOOTING

- **Yellow drooping leaves** Most likely onion fly. Pull and burn affected plants.
- **Orange-brown blotches** Probably rust. Pull and burn affected plants.
- **Dark green drooping leaves** Too much nitrogen. Only use well-rotted manure.

Parsnips

Parsnips are fully hardy, they are easy to grow, they will thrive in just about any well-prepared, fertile soil and they can be left in the ground over winter. They are incredibly delicious when served up on the plate, whether roasted in the oven with potatoes or steamed and mashed.

SOW											HARVEST											
Jan	Feb	Mar	Apr	May	Jun	Jul	Aug	Sep	Oct	Nov	Dec	Jan	Feb	Mar	Apr	May	Jun	Jul	Aug	Sep	Oct	Nov	Dec

White King

A classic long-rooting variety for deep soil. It produces tapered, medium-sized, creamy-skinned and white-fleshed roots. The texture is firm and the flavour nutty.

More varieties

- **Avon Resister** Short, tapered, canker-resistant variety. This one is a good option if your soil is poor, shallow and stony.

- **F1 Countess** Disease-tolerant, high-yielding, maincrop variety that produces smooth-skinned roots. This is a good choice if you want to show your crop for shape and texture.

- **F1 Gladiator** Canker-resistant variety for a deep soil. It produces smooth-skinned, larger-than-average roots – bigger than most other varieties. A good choice if you are trying to grow the biggest vegetables.

- **Hollow Crown** Reliable variety for a deep soil. It produces long, tapered, white-skinned, creamy-fleshed roots.

SOIL AND SITE NEEDS

Parsnips will do well on just about any well-prepared, friable, fine-textured, well-drained, fertile soil. If the soil has been dug to a good depth – so that the roots can go straight down without obstruction – and if it has been well manured for a preceding crop, then parsnips will thrive. They do not like fresh manure, however; as with carrots, if the growing roots hit fresh manure they will either fork or become cankered. If you have no real choice other than to grow parsnips on poor, stony soil, then it is best to opt for one of the short, stubby varieties.

SOWING AND PLANTING PROCEDURES

- Sow seeds from mid-February to the end of April; run 1.5 cm (½ in) deep drills 20–25 cm (8–10 in) apart. Sow 3–4 seeds together at 13–15 cm (5–6 in) intervals.
- Compact the soil over the seeds and water them generously with a fine spray. Be careful not to 'puddle' the area.
- When the seedlings can be handled, thin each group to the strongest plant.

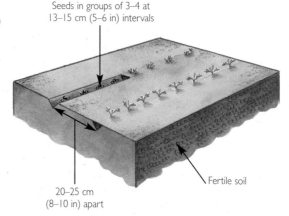

Seeds in groups of 3–4 at 13–15 cm (5–6 in) intervals

20–25 cm (8–10 in) apart

Fertile soil

PLANT CARE

Stir the surface of the soil with a hoe in order to create a loose-soil mulch. Be very careful when doing this that you do not scuff or graze the emerging root; such damage often results in top-rot or canker. Water little and often so as to avoid wet-drought-wet conditions that result in root splitting.

HARVESTING

You can harvest from October through to March. Parsnips are unaffected by frost, so you can leave them in the ground until needed. When you come to lifting, ease them up with a fork, being careful not to break off the long root tips.

TROUBLESHOOTING

- **Parsnip canker** Shows itself as a rusty brown area around the 'shoulders' and is usually caused by physical damage to the root and/or contact with fresh manure. Only use well-rotted manure and do not touch the roots with the hoe.
- **Fanging** A forked root caused by the presence of fresh manure and/or lots of stones. Try to avoid both.

Peas

Most people like fresh-picked peas, which are very high in protein and natural sugar. Meat-eaters often favour them served alongside roast lamb; vegetarians eat them with just about everything; and even 'no-veg' children will eat them. They are an essential ingredient of any allotment.

SOW		HARVEST																					
Jan	Feb	Mar	Apr	May	Jun	Jul	Aug	Sep	Oct	Nov	Dec	Jan	Feb	Mar	Apr	May	Jun	Jul	Aug	Sep	Oct	Nov	Dec

Alderman
A traditional, tall-growing, maincrop variety, to 1–1.5 m (3–5 ft) high, that produces masses of large pods. The peas are firm and flavoursome – everything you would expect from a traditional pea.

More varieties
- **Avola** Reliable, low-growing, heavy-cropping, first early variety, producing good-sized, sweet, tasty peas that are much better than shop-bought ones.
- **Greenshaft** Very popular, low-growing, heavy-cropping, second early variety, growing to about 60 cm (2 ft) high. It produces masses of long, pointed pods that grow in pairs.
- **Lincoln** Reliable maincrop variety, growing to about 60 cm (2 ft) high. It produces an abundance of dark green, slightly curved pods. Characteristic firm texture and sweet taste.
- **Norli** Mangetout variety bearing masses of flat, medium-green, stringless pods. Good choice if you enjoy mangetout types.

SOIL AND SITE NEEDS

Although peas will grow on any well-prepared, deeply worked, moist soil, early crops do best on warm, dry, sandy soil and main crops prefer a heavier, richer, moisture-retentive loam. The key words here are 'deeply worked'. If the manure is fresh or there is too much of it, the peas will tend to roar out of control and become all leaf with too few pods. Peas need large amounts of moisture. If at any time you see the ground around the plants cracking or drying out, soak it with water and then cover the ground with a mulch of old, well-rotted, spent manure.

SOWING AND PLANTING PROCEDURES

- Sow seeds in succession from March to July in drills 5 cm (2 in) deep and 38–120 cm (15–48 in) apart, depending upon the variety. Space seeds 13–15 cm (5–6 in) apart.
- Compact the soil and water generously.
- Cover the rows with wire mesh, twigs, muslin – anything to keep the birds away.
- Watch out for pigeons, rabbits, mice and cats, which can all be a problem.

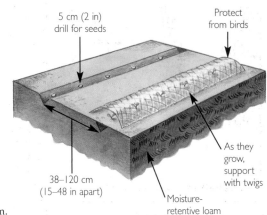

5 cm (2 in) drill for seeds

Protect from birds

As they grow, support with twigs

38–120 cm (15–48 in apart)

Moisture-retentive loam

PLANT CARE

As soon as the seedlings appear, stir the surface of the soil with a hoe to create a fine, loose soil mulch. Repeat this hoeing at least every week throughout the season, especially in dry weather. In long dry, spells, drench the soil with water and put a heaped line of old manure mulch on each side of the row.

HARVESTING

You can harvest from June through to October. Peas tend to swell rapidly, so make a point of gathering them when they are still young. Remember to pick the pods every 2–3 days, as this will encourage new ones to develop.

TROUBLESHOOTING

- **Aphids** Large colonies of aphids generally stunt growth. Remove affected areas and spray with a mix of water and liquid soap.
- **Mould and mildew** Show themselves as yellow leaves and/or white patches, usually in dry weather. Save what you can of the peas and burn the plants.
- **Pea moth** Little maggots appear within the pod. Eat what you can and try a different variety the next time around.

Potatoes

Shop-bought potatoes are very cheap and plentiful, but there is nothing like the pleasure of digging and eating your own. From new potatoes served up with mint and a dab of butter to those eaten roast, mashed, fried or cold, home-grown potatoes are always special.

	PLANT				**HARVEST**																		
Jan	Feb	Mar	Apr	May	Jun	Jul	Aug	Sep	Oct	Nov	Dec	Jan	Feb	Mar	Apr	May	Jun	Jul	Aug	Sep	Oct	Nov	Dec

Desiree
A very popular, drought-resistant, early main variety. It produces a heavy yield of medium-sized, shiny, red-skinned, creamy-fleshed tubers with a smooth texture and a sweet taste.

Marfona
A high-yielding, second early variety. It produces large, smooth-skinned tubers. This is the one to choose if you enjoy roast potatoes or baked jacket potatoes.

King Edward
A popular and well-known, early main variety known for its texture and taste. It produces a heavy crop of pink/cream-skinned, creamy-fleshed tubers.

More varieties

- **Charlotte:** A reliable, high-yielding salad variety. It produces medium-sized, waxy-textured tubers.

- **Estima:** A popular, heavy-cropping, second early, Dutch variety.

- **Maris Piper:** An eelworm-resistant, maincrop variety that is good for making chips (French fries).

- **Nicola:** A late main salad variety that produces long, waxy-fleshed tubers.

- **Princess:** A popular, mid-season variety that produces yellow-skinned, firm, yellow-fleshed tubers.

SOIL AND SITE NEEDS

Potatoes are easy to grow in just about any soil. The very act of earthing them up, and lifting them, has a cleansing effect on the soil, so they are a very good starter crop for a new allotment, and it is a good idea to grow as many as possible. The site should be open to full sun and, if you want to avoid unpleasant, serious diseases such as potato blight, it should also be one on which potatoes were not grown during the previous season.

Although just about any soil will support potatoes, the character of the soil does, to a great extent, decide the texture, colour and flavour of the cooked potato. For example, a heavy, wet soil tends to result in a slick, soapy, slightly yellow potato, whereas potatoes grown on dry, sandy soil are often loose and fluffy. A damp, badly drained or low-lying soil will produce good potatoes in a hot, dry year, but if the weather is extra hot and humid they will be the first to show problems. Ideally, the soil needs to be deeply dug, well-drained, friable, clay to sandy, and moisture-retentive.

SOWING AND PLANTING PROCEDURES

- Chitting for early crop (February) – sit the seed potatoes in trays in a shed, until there are 2.5 cm (1 in) long shoots growing out of them.
- Sowing early (March–April) – dig 15 cm (6 in) deep drills, and set the chitted seeds 30–40 cm (12–16 in) apart, in rows 60–75 cm (24–30 in) apart.
- Cover the shoots with soil. Be extremely careful when you are doing this that you do not cause any damage – with the hoe – to the side of the tuber.
- If the weather is cold, protect the newly covered shoots with straw and fleece.
- Sowing under black plastic (March–April) – rake and water the soil. Set the chitted seeds

on the surface, 30–40 cm (12–16 in) apart, in rows that are 60–75 cm (24–30 in) apart. Rake a long mound of soil over the potatoes and cover with black plastic sheet that is 90 cm (3 ft) wide. Cut slits at each planting point for the potato plants to grow through.

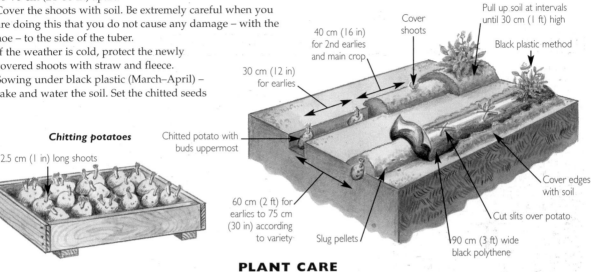

Chitting potatoes

2.5 cm (1 in) long shoots

Chitted potato with buds uppermost

30 cm (12 in) for earlies

40 cm (16 in) for 2nd earlies and main crop

Cover shoots

Pull up soil at intervals until 30 cm (1 ft) high

Black plastic method

60 cm (2 ft) for earlies to 75 cm (30 in) according to variety

Slug pellets

90 cm (3 ft) wide black polythene

Cut slits over potato

Cover edges with soil

PLANT CARE

As soon as the foliage shows, use a hoe to draw the soil up to form a ridge. Repeat this procedure as necessary so that the foliage is always just showing at the top of the ridge. Although you always need to be aware that if you cover the haulms with more than 15 cm (6 in) of soil the crop will be held back, you must make sure that all the small potatoes are covered with soil.

In very hot weather, stir the surface of the soil with a hoe to create a loose-soil mulch. Always be on the lookout for slugs. If the weather is very dry, spread a mulch of spent manure or chopped straw around the plants.

If you are using the black polythene method, roll back the plastic in early June, remove any slugs, check for general condition, and replace the plastic.

TROUBLESHOOTING

← **Cutworms** *These are the caterpillar stage of various moths, and damage shows as holes and tunnels in the potatoes. To avoid further problems with cutworms, grow the crop on a different plot the next time around.*

← **Cyst eelworms** *These pests live in the tubers, and show as wilting and rotting foliage. Destroy infected plants and grow resistant varieties on new ground.*

↙ **Potato blight** *Shows as brown, sickly-looking leaves. This is a very serious disease. Grow disease-resistant varieties on another plot, and be sure to keep any infected potatoes well away from tomatoes. Remove and burn infected plants.*

HARVESTING

You can harvest potatoes from June right through to October. It is best to use a broad-tined, flat-pronged or blob-pronged fork. Dig deep and gradually work from the outer limits of the plant towards the centre. Try not to damage the potatoes. Leave the potatoes on the surface until the end of the session, and then sort and bag them up into 'good' ones and 'damaged' ones. Eat the damaged ones first. Lift new potatoes as needed.

Store surplus maincrop potatoes in shallow boxes in a dry, dark, frost-free shed, or outside on a piece of high ground in a clamp. To build a clamp, let the potatoes dry, pile them up into a long, ridge-shaped heap, and then cover the heap with straw topped with a 15 cm (6 in) layer of earth. Dig a trench around the clamp – like a moat – and channel off any standing water.

Radishes

When I was at infant school, I scratched my initials out in a patch of earth, sprinkled in radish seeds, watched them grow, and then, best of all, ate them in sandwiches. Radishes can be grown from packet to plate in four weeks, and they are perfect with bread and cheese.

Jan	Feb	Mar	Apr	May	Jun	Jul	Aug	Sep	Oct	Nov	Dec	Jan	Feb	Mar	Apr	May	Jun	Jul	Aug	Sep	Oct	Nov	Dec

SOW — HARVEST

French Breakfast

One of the oldest and most popular spring and summer varieties. It produces a long, red, white-tipped root, and is a good choice if you want something to munch with your lettuce sandwiches.

More varieties

- **Cherry Belle:** A mild-flavoured spring and summer variety that produces bright red, cherry-like, white-fleshed roots. The texture, bite and taste are perfect for a salad.

- **Pink Beauty:** A fast-growing variety with red-to-pink roots. The white flesh is tender and very flavoursome.

- **Scarlet Globe:** A popular, quick-growing, early-cropping, traditional variety. It produces beautiful, tight, round, red roots with a crisp texture and a delicate to mild flavour.

- **Sparkler:** A reliable, easy-to-grow variety. It produces spherical roots that are scarlet at the top and white at the bottom with a crisp, crunchy texture and a good flavour.

SOIL AND SITE NEEDS

Radishes do best on rich, moist, fertile soil in a sunny position. Ideally, the soil needs to be porous, easily worked, friable and rich in humus from previous crops. They do well on soil made up from well-broken, sifted and semi-exhausted manure-peat compost gathered from hotbeds, growing-bags and so on. Stay away from soil that is rich in fresh manure as it will result in fast-growing, leafy plants that are small, tough and stringy at the root – they look good but there is nothing to eat. Choose a sunny, open spot. Make sure that you compact the surface of the soil before and after sowing, so that the roots plump up, as loose soil results in thin, scraggy roots.

SOWING AND PLANTING PROCEDURES

- Every few days in succession from January to August – sow seeds 12 mm (½ in) deep in drills 10–15 cm (4–6 in) apart. Compact the soil and water generously.
- When the seedlings are big enough to handle, thin to leave the strongest plants 2.5 cm (1 in) apart. Warning: some people are allergic to the touch of the leaves – it brings their hands up in a rash.
- Water generously before and after thinning.

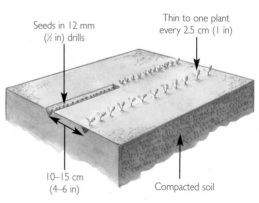

Seeds in 12 mm (½ in) drills

Thin to one plant every 2.5 cm (1 in)

10–15 cm (4–6 in)

Compacted soil

PLANT CARE

Stir the surface of the soil with a hoe at each side of the row to create a loose-soil mulch. Water little and often, so as to avoid the wet/drought/wet conditions that result in root splitting. If the weather is very dry, hoe a mulch of spent manure up against each side of the row.

HARVESTING

You can harvest from April to February, depending upon the variety and growing methods. Pull them when they are small, young and tender – the size depends upon the variety. Eat them as soon as possible after pulling.

TROUBLESHOOTING

- **Slugs and snails** Show as holes in leaves and damage to the roots. Slugs and snails can halt the growth of the young plants. Gather the pests by hand.
- **Big foliage and little roots** Lots of lush foliage with small, woody roots point to there being too much nitrogen in the soil – probably rank manure. Avoid the problem by only using well-rotted manure.

Salsify and scorzonera

If you enjoy growing and eating root crops such as parsnips and turnips, then salsify and its close relative scorzonera will also be a good choice for you to grow on your allotment. They do not look especially pretty on a plate, but they crop heavily and are very tasty.

| SOW | | | | | | | | | | HARVEST | | | | | | | | | | | | |
|Jan|Feb|Mar|Apr|May|Jun|Jul|Aug|Sep|Oct|Nov|Dec|Jan|Feb|Mar|Apr|May|Jun|Jul|Aug|Sep|Oct|Nov|Dec|

Sandwich Island
A traditional, easy-grow salsify variety that was popular in the 1900s, when it was grown by market gardeners for well-to-do private customers and high-class hotels. It produces long, thin, brown, white-fleshed, parsnip-like roots.

More varieties
- **Giant French:** An old salsify variety, popular in England in the 1900s, when people thought the taste and texture of salsify and scorzonera went well together. If you damage the roots, they will bleed and lose their flavour.

- **Large Black:** An easy-grow scorzonera variety, sometimes known as Giant Black or even Giant Russian. It produces a very large, purple-black root, much the same as Long Black Maxima, but not quite so long. The taste and texture are good.

- **Long Black Maxima:** A heavy-yielding, bolt-resistant scorzonera variety. It produces very long, dark brown roots that are not pretty, but very flavoursome.

SOIL AND SITE NEEDS

Salsify and scorzonera produce the biggest, longest roots in a deep, light-textured, moist, fertile soil. They will grow in a heavy soil, however, providing it is deeply worked until it is fine-textured, friable and free from stones. As with carrots and parsnips, the roots tend to waver and weaken if they come across stones. The soil must be thoroughly prepared with lots of well-rotted manure. Avoid digging in fresh manure, as it will cause the roots to divide and possibly rot, and also result in the flavour being a bit rank and muddy.

SOWING AND PLANTING PROCEDURES

- April–May – create 12 mm (½ in) deep drills, 25–30 cm (10–12 in) apart, and sow a pinch of 2–3 seeds at 13–15 cm (5–6 in) intervals.
- Compact the soil and use a fine spray to water generously.
- When the seedlings are big enough to handle, pinch out to leave the strongest plant every 15 cm (6 in).
- Water before and after thinning out, and firm the earth up around all the remaining plants.

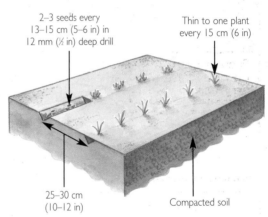

2–3 seeds every 13–15 cm (5–6 in) in 12 mm (½ in) deep drill

Thin to one plant every 15 cm (6 in)

25–30 cm (10–12 in)

Compacted soil

PLANT CARE

Stir the surface of the soil with a hoe to create a loose-soil mulch. As with parsnips and turnips, be careful not to scuff the emerging shoulder, as such damage often results in top-rot or canker. Water a little and often to avoid wet/drought/wet conditions that result in the root splitting.

HARVESTING

You can harvest from October to April. Lift and eat as needed. A good option with a large crop is to chop the old tops off in autumn, hoe soil over to a depth of 13–15 cm (5–6 in), and then eat the resulting blanched shoots the following spring.

TROUBLESHOOTING

- **Blistered leaves** Show as masses of shiny, white spores on the leaves, and results in slow, uneven growth. The problem can usually be halted by pulling and burning affected plants, so that remaining plants are well spaced.
- **Root damage** Shows itself as scabrous, orange-brown stains to the top of the roots, just like parsnip canker. Usually caused by hoeing damage.

Spinach

Many people find spinach unappetizing, but this is because it is usually overcooked. When it is freshly picked, steamed for a few minutes, well drained, and served with bread and butter, it is absolutely delicious. Better still, it can be grown all year round.

			SOW						HARVEST														
Jan	Feb	Mar	Apr	May	Jun	Jul	Aug	Sep	Oct	Nov	Dec	Jan	Feb	Mar	Apr	May	Jun	Jul	Aug	Sep	Oct	Nov	Dec

Matador

A reliable, easy-grow, semi-erect, early variety that has attractive, large, green, rubbery-looking leaves with good texture and taste.

More varieties

- **Atlanta:** A very reliable, summer- and autumn-cropping variety with thick, dark green, fleshy, lettuce-like leaves that are succulent and tasty.

- **Bloomsdale:** A heavy-yielding, bolt-resistant, summer variety with an abundance of dark green leaves.

- **Giant Thick Leaved Prickly:** A winter- and spring-cropping variety with huge, dark green leaves with a crisp texture and distinctive taste.

- **Giant Winter:** A very reliable, hardy, winter variety that produces a mass of large, dark green leaves with a crisp texture and full taste.

- **Medania:** A slow-bolting, spring-cropping variety with a smoother taste than some larger varieties.

SOIL AND SITE NEEDS

Spinach can be relatively easily grown on almost any soil. This is borne out by the fact that traditionally it was grown swiftly as a catch crop in the space between other vegetables. In one way, it does not matter if the soil is a bit thin or dry, and the crop bolts, because it can be swiftly cropped and cleared in the space of a few weeks, and then just as swiftly resown. While spinach will grow just about anywhere, it will only produce big, fat, plump leaves if the soil is well prepared, well manured and moisture-retentive, and the crop is planted so that there is plenty of room between rows.

SOWING AND PLANTING PROCEDURES

- March–June – create 2.5 cm (1 in) deep drills, 25–30 cm (10–12 in) apart. Sow seeds thinly and cover.
- Compact the soil and use a fine spray to water generously.
- When the seedlings are big enough to handle, first pinch out to leave the strongest plants 7.5 cm (3 in) apart, and then later, when the leaves touch, thin out to 15 cm (6 in) apart.
- Water before and after thinning, and eat the thinnings.

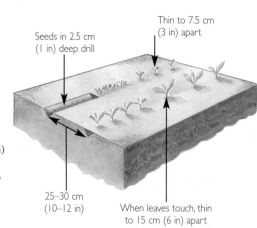

Seeds in 2.5 cm (1 in) deep drill

Thin to 7.5 cm (3 in) apart

25–30 cm (10–12 in)

When leaves touch, thin to 15 cm (6 in) apart

PLANT CARE

Stir the surface of the soil with a hoe to create a loose-soil mulch. Water liberally. If the weather becomes dry, spread a generous layer of spent manure mulch along both sides of the row and keep watering. A shortage of water will result in premature bolting.

HARVESTING

You can harvest from May to the following April – most of the year – depending upon the variety and growing methods. Pick the leaves by hand, all the time keeping the plants in good condition by breaking off old and tired leaves.

TROUBLESHOOTING

- **Distorted leaves** Probably spinach blight, a disease caused by a virus and spread by aphids. Wash aphids off with a liquid soap and water solution, and pull and burn badly affected plants.
- **Mouldy leaves** Probably downy mildew. Avoid the problem by generous spacing, so that there is plenty of airflow between the plants.

Swedes

Swedes are easy to grow as well as perfectly delicious to eat. During my childhood, when I heard my grandfather describe our next meal as 'bashed and buttered', I knew that we were in for a tasty treat of mashed swede with bread and butter.

| Jan | Feb | Mar | Apr | **SOW** May | Jun | Jul | Aug | Sep | Oct | Nov | **HARVEST** Dec | Jan | Feb | Mar | Apr | May | Jun | Jul | Aug | Sep | Oct | Nov | Dec |

Marian

A very hardy, vigorous and productive, disease-resistant variety. It produces large, purple-skinned, yellow-fleshed roots with a good taste.

More varieties

- **Angela:** A new, early-cropping variety that produces medium to large, purple-skinned, creamy-fleshed roots with a good, even flavour.
- **Best of All:** A very hardy and productive variety. It produces large, purple-topped, yellow-fleshed roots.
- **Purple Top:** A very popular and reliable, tried and trusted, old variety. It produces firm-textured roots that are good for mashing and store well.

SOIL AND SITE NEEDS

Swedes do best on a soil that ranges from being a light, rich loam to a sandy loam, the proviso being that the soil is moisture-retentive and fed with plenty of well-rotted manure. The soil needs to be deeply worked and, above all, moist, because if it dries the plants will bolt without bulbing. Avoid ground that looks to be sticky and/or 'puddled' with standing water. Swedes do best in an open, semi-shaded position with shelter on the windward side.

SOWING AND PLANTING PROCEDURES

- April–June – create 12 mm (½ in) deep drills, 25–30 cm (10–12 in) apart; sow seeds, compact the soil and use a fine spray to water generously.
- When the seedlings are big enough to handle, pinch out to leave the strongest plants 7.5 cm (3 in) apart. Later, when the leaves start to touch, thin the plants out again to 15 cm (6 in) apart.
- Water after thinning, and use your finger to firm the soil up around the remaining plants.

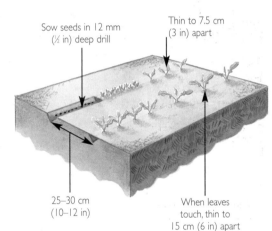

Sow seeds in 12 mm (½ in) deep drill

Thin to 7.5 cm (3 in) apart

25–30 cm (10–12 in)

When leaves touch, thin to 15 cm (6 in) apart

PLANT CARE

Stir the surface of the soil with a hoe to create a loose-soil mulch. Be very careful that you do not graze the emerging root, as such damage might well result in top-rot or canker. Water a little and often so as to avoid the flood/drought/flood conditions that cause root splitting.

HARVESTING

You can harvest from September to March. Lift the roots as needed. They are best when eaten small, young and tender. Store any surplus roots by twisting off the leaves and then burying them in peat in plastic dustbins.

TROUBLESHOOTING

- **Slugs and snails** Show as holes in leaves and damage to the roots. Slugs and snails can halt the growth of the young plants. Gather the pests by hand.
- **Big foliage and little roots** Lots of lush foliage with small, woody roots point to there being too much nitrogen in the soil – probably rank manure. Avoid the problem by only using well-rotted manure.

Sweetcorn

When I was first gardening in the early 1960s, sweetcorn was thought to be a wonderfully exotic item that could only thrive in the extreme south of England. The good news is that modern varieties have pushed the no-grow line in the UK as far north as the Scottish borders.

| Jan | Feb | Mar | Apr | May | Jun | Jul | Aug | Sep | Oct | Nov | Dec | Jan | Feb | Mar | Apr | May | Jun | Jul | Aug | Sep | Oct | Nov | Dec |

SOW ▼ (May)   HARVEST ▼ (Aug/Sep)

FI Sweet Nugget
A reliable, outdoor, September-cropping variety that is a very good choice for cooler conditions. It produces medium-long cobs with large, sweet-tasting, golden kernels.

More varieties

• **FI Minipop:** A miniature variety that produces very small cobs that can be eaten raw in salads or cooked.

• **FI Tasty Gold:** A super-sweet, September-cropping variety that produces 23–25 cm (9–10 in) long cobs with large, golden kernels. It needs a lot of moisture to ensure germination.

• **FI Tuxedo:** A tall, disease-tolerant, sugar-enhanced variety that produces 23–25 cm (9–10 in) long cobs with well-fattened kernels. Be aware when you are ordering seed that there are now three types – normal sugar, sugar-enhanced and super-sweet. It is important, to avoid cross-pollination between the types, that you grow them well away from each other.

SOIL AND SITE NEEDS

Sweetcorn likes a well-prepared, deeply worked, well-drained, light to sandy soil in a sheltered, sunny position. Dig plenty of manure and compost in during the autumn so that it is well rotted by the time it comes to plant. Sweetcorn needs lots of moisture. If you see the ground drying out, soak it with water and cover the ground with a mulch of well-rotted spent manure. As to varieties, there is no problem if you live in the south where you can plant just about any variety that takes your fancy; but if you live further north and are worried about difficult conditions, it is best to try a variety like Northern Xtra Sweet that can withstand cold winds.

SOWING AND PLANTING PROCEDURES

• Late April–early May – sow one chitted seed per peat pot under glass or plastic, and water generously.

• Mid-May–mid-June – a few days prior to planting, harden the plants off by standing them outside in a sheltered, sunny position. Dig holes to fit the peat pots – 30–45 cm (12–18 in) apart in a grid pattern – and use a fine spray to water the plants into place.

Put plants in their peat pots in the holes

Make holes in a grid pattern 30–45 cm (12–18 in) apart

Protect cobs with netting

PLANT CARE

Stir the surface of the soil with a hoe to create a loose-soil mulch. Drag the soil up to support the stems. Be careful not to damage the stems when the plants are at the young and fragile stage. In dry weather, when the flowers are finished, water and cover the ground with a thick mulch. Protect with a net when the cobs start to show.

HARVESTING

You can harvest from July to October. The cobs are ready when the tail-like silks are almost black-brown and when the grains ooze a milky fluid under pressure. Pick the cobs by hand, with a swift twist-and-down action.

TROUBLESHOOTING

• **Distorted seedlings** Show as distorted leaves, general weak growth and small, white maggots inside the young shoots, caused by the frit fly. Avoid by growing seedlings under cover until they are beyond the five-leaf stage.

• **Mushroom-like growths** Show as growths on the cob, caused by 'smut' infection. Pull and burn at the first sign of a problem and rotate the crops.

Tomatoes (under cover)

One look around your local allotment will bear witness to the fact that holders delight in building DIY greenhouses, out of old windows and such like, just so that they can grow tomatoes. You can also grow them under other forms of protection such as cloches or polytunnels.

SOW	PLANT				HARVEST																		
Jan	Feb	Mar	Apr	May	Jun	Jul	Aug	Sep	Oct	Nov	Dec	Jan	Feb	Mar	Apr	May	Jun	Jul	Aug	Sep	Oct	Nov	Dec

Harbinger

An early-cropping variety that is just right for growing under unheated protection. It produces a heavy crop of good-sized, sweet-tasting tomatoes.

More varieties

- **Beefsteak:** A good, tall-growing, under-cover variety that produces large, pinky-red fruits.

- **F1 Big Boy:** A large-fruit variety. This is the one to choose if you enjoy huge tomatoes – for stuffing or slicing in sandwiches.

- **Sun Baby:** An intermediate variety that is good for growing outdoors or under cover. It produces small, yellow, cherry-like fruits.

- **Sunbelle:** A small, yellow-fruit variety with very sweet flavour and tender skins. Good for a growing-bag.

SOIL AND SITE NEEDS

In the context of an allotment, the term 'under cover' usually means some sort of cobbled-up 'greenhouse' such as a plastic screen or a tall cloche made from salvaged windows. The easiest way of growing tomatoes in this way is to grow them directly in a growing-bag. You simply sit the bag in a sheltered, sunny position, sort out the supports and a shelter of plastic sheeting or whatever you have chosen, and then get on with the sowing and planting. Grown in this set-up, all you have to worry about is the watering. The rule of thumb for watering is as much as possible as long as the water does not 'puddle' around the plants. If you remember that tomatoes hate irregular watering and stagnant water, then you will not go far wrong.

SOWING AND PLANTING PROCEDURES

- End February–mid-March – sow the seeds in a tray on a bed of moistened potting compost, and protect with a sheet of glass topped with newspaper.
- April–May – when the seedlings are large enough, prick them out into 7.5 cm (3 in) peat pots. Water and keep warm.
- May–June – set the peat pots in growing-bags, water generously and protect with the cloche or plastic shelter of your choice.

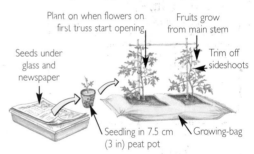

Plant on when flowers on first truss start opening

Fruits grow from main stem

Seeds under glass and newspaper

Trim off sideshoots

Seedling in 7.5 cm (3 in) peat pot

Growing-bag

PLANT CARE

Support the plant with a cane or stake and loose ties. Pinch out the sideshoots that grow from the angle between leaf and stem. Remove the growing point just short of the top of the shelter. Water growing-bags little and often, with a dedicated liquid feed in the water. Remove yellow foliage.

HARVESTING

You can harvest from June to October, depending upon the variety and growing methods. When the first bunch of fruits is beginning to ripen, you can speed up the process by stripping off all the leaves from the ground to the first leaf above the bunch. Pluck the tomatoes when they are firm and nicely coloured.

TROUBLESHOOTING

- **Dropping flowers** Caused by dry conditions. The problem can be avoided by frequent watering.
- **Discoloured fruits** Show as patchy, green-black skin. Caused by shortage of water at the early stage.
- **Bronze colour** Shows as brown patches just under the surface of the skin, and results in poor growth. Caused by a virus. Avoid by using virus-resistant plants.

Tomatoes (outdoors)

A great deal will depend upon where you live and the location of your plot – its orientation, the soil type, the prevailing winds and so on – but if you can find a sheltered, sunny corner then you can usually grow tomatoes successfully in the open allotment.

SOW		PLANT			HARVEST																		
Jan	Feb	Mar	Apr	May	Jun	Jul	Aug	Sep	Oct	Nov	Dec	Jan	Feb	Mar	Apr	May	Jun	Jul	Aug	Sep	Oct	Nov	Dec

Gartenperle

An early-cropping, bush-type variety that is good for growing in hanging-baskets or containers. It produces masses of small, cherry-like fruits.

More varieties

- **Marmande:** A very popular, late-maturing variety. It produces large, uneven fruits with a beautiful flavour.

- **Moneymaker:** One of the most popular and reliable, heavy-cropping varieties of all. It produces masses of small to medium-sized fruits.

- **St Pierre:** A traditional, French, late-cropping variety that produces small to medium-sized fruits.

- **The Amateur:** A tried-and-trusted bush variety that produces full-flavoured, medium-sized fruits. It is a good choice if this is your first attempt at growing tomatoes.

SOIL AND SITE NEEDS

In many ways, outdoor tomatoes can stand just about any soil from light and sandy to heavy clay, as long as it is deeply worked, richly manured, compact, well drained and in a sunny, sheltered position. The deeply dug soil provides moisture when the weather is dry.

SOWING AND PLANTING PROCEDURES

- End March–mid-April – sow the seeds in a tray on a bed of moistened potting compost, and protect with a sheet of glass topped with newspaper. Keep warm.
- Late May – when the seedlings are large enough, prick them out into 7.5 cm (3 in) peat pots. Water and keep warm.

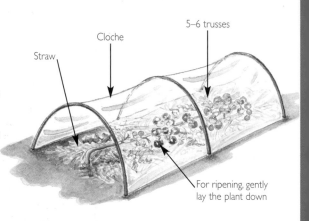

Straw

Cloche

5–6 trusses

For ripening, gently lay the plant down

- May–June – set the peat pots in place in a sheltered position, water generously and protect with the cloche or plastic shelter of your choice.

PLANT CARE

Support the plant with a stake and loose ties. Pinch out the sideshoots. Remove the growing tip when there are 5–6 trusses. When the fruits start to ripen, cover the ground with a mulch of rotted manure topped with a bed of straw, remove the supports and gently lay the plant down. Cover with the cloche and continue to water the roots.

HARVESTING

You can harvest from July to October, depending upon the variety. When the first bunch of fruits is beginning to ripen, strip off all the leaves to the first leaf above the bunch, and remove damaged fruit. Check that the straw is crisp and dry. Pluck the tomatoes when they are firm and nicely coloured.

TROUBLESHOOTING

- **Discoloured leaves** Caused by one of many viruses. Show as curled, splotchy-brown leaves. Pull and burn all badly affected plants. Avoid the problem by using virus-resistant varieties.
- **Blight** Shows itself as rotten fruit. Pull and burn affected plants. Grow on another plot the next time. Do not follow the tomatoes on with potatoes.

Turnips

Some people may be put off by memories of school-dinner turnips, but home-grown turnips are a world apart – so tender and tasty that they can be eaten raw, or roasted, or in any way that takes your fancy. Turnip tops, sown in autumn and ready in spring, can be eaten as spring greens.

SOW Depending on variety HARVEST

Jan	Feb	Mar	Apr	May	Jun	Jul	Aug	Sep	Oct	Nov	Dec	Jan	Feb	Mar	Apr	May	Jun	Jul	Aug	Sep	Oct	Nov	Dec

Milan Purple Top

A very attractive, fast-maturing, early variety that produces a flat, purple-topped, white-fleshed root.

More varieties

- **F1 Market Express:** A fast-growing, spring- and early summer-sowing variety. It produces spherical, white roots with a firm texture and fine flavour. It reaches maturity about 50 days after sowing.

- **Golden Ball:** A popular, spring-sowing variety. It produces sweet-tasting, golden, firm-fleshed roots, and reaches maturity in the space of about three months.

- **Green Top Stone:** A popular and reliable, autumn-sowing variety that produces smallish, green-white roots with a firm texture and delicate taste.

SOIL AND SITE NEEDS

Turnips, just like swedes, do well on a rich, light, sandy, moisture-retentive loam. If you have a choice between a sticky clay or dry, sandy soil, then opt for the sand and make adjustments. The soil needs to be deeply worked, well manured with rotted compost and, above all, moist, because if it dries outs the roots will falter and the plants will bolt and come to nothing. Avoid ground that looks to be sticky and/or 'puddled' with standing water. Turnips do best in an open, semi-shaded position with shelter on the windward side.

SOWING AND PLANTING PROCEDURES

- February–June or July–September, depending upon variety – create 12 mm (½ in) deep drills, 25–30 cm (10–12 in) apart; sow seeds thinly and cover.
- Compact the soil and water generously.
- When the seedlings are big enough to handle, first pinch out to leave the strongest plants 7.5 cm (3 in) apart, and then later thin to 15 cm (6 in) apart.
- Water before and after thinning. Use your fingers to firm the soil up around the young plants.

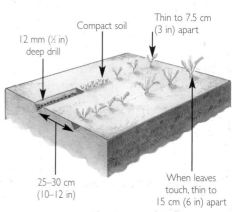

Compact soil

12 mm (½ in) deep drill

Thin to 7.5 cm (3 in) apart

25–30 cm (10–12 in)

When leaves touch, thin to 15 cm (6 in) apart

PLANT CARE

Stir the surface of the soil with a hoe to create a loose-soil mulch. Be careful not to damage the turnips' 'shoulders', as this might result in top-rot or canker. Water a little and often. If there is a do-or-die drought, give the ground one good, slow soaking and top it off with a thick mulch.

HARVESTING

You can, depending on the variety, harvest the roots from October to the end of December, and the tops from March to April. Lift the roots as needed. Turnips are best when they are eaten small, young and tender. To store surplus roots, twist off the leaves and bury the roots in peat in plastic dustbins.

TROUBLESHOOTING

- **Slugs and snails** Show as holes in leaves and damage to the roots. Slugs and snails can halt the growth of the young plants. Gather the pests by hand.
- **Canker** Shows itself as a rusty brown area around the 'shoulders' – usually caused by physical damage to the root, and/or contact with fresh manure. Only use well-rotted manure, and be careful not to touch the roots with the hoe.

Getting started

Much depends on how much time and effort you are intending to put in, whether you start with bare-rooted or container-grown plants, and whether you are prepared to build screens and other aids. With soft or cane fruits, such as blackberries, currants and strawberries, you can expect a crop in the space of a year; with tree fruits, such as apples, pears and plums, you can be eating the produce in two or three years.

What is a fruit?

The term 'fruit' is botanically defined as 'the ripened ovary of a flowering plant, containing one or more seeds'. The term is rather confusing in that gardeners and cooks think of some fruits, such as tomatoes, as being vegetables. I have decided to stick with the old definition that declares 'if it is sweet and juicy, and generally served up raw or cooked as a dessert or pudding, and if we eat it variously dunked, dipped or covered in sugar, custard, cream, ice cream or yogurt, then it is a fruit'.

Looking around other people's allotments will show you that growing small fruit trees is a popular option, because they are relatively easy to grow and very productive.

Redcurrants can be grown as a bush in the open ground, as a pot plant, or stretched along wires as a cordon. The fruits not only look attractive, but they are also tasty and nutritious.

HOW TO BEGIN

There are two possibilities – you can start with soft fruits such as strawberries, and then gradually work through the bush and cane fruits such as raspberries and gooseberries, and finally go for the tree fruits such as apples and pears, or you can sort out the apples and pears first. My advice is to hold back with the trees for the first year. If you spend the first year getting established – generally sorting out what goes where and how – you will have a better understanding of your needs and can adapt your plot accordingly.

PESTS AND DISEASES

Prevention is always better than cure. Ask neighbouring plot-holders what does best for them. Choose tried-and-trusted, disease-resistant varieties, choose the planting area with care (the right soil, sunlight and air-flow conditions), prepare the ground as advised, avoid overcrowding, and generally take time and trouble at every stage. This should keep problems to a minimum.

Apples

More and more allotment-holders are planting apple trees. If you plant a container-grown 2–3-year-old dwarf or bush tree, it will show its first fruits about one year after planting and then give you a good crop in the second year.

PLANT BARE-ROOTED (Plant container-grown any time)											**PRUNE**						**HARVEST**			
Jan	Feb	Mar	Apr	May	Jun	Jul	Aug	Sep	Oct	Nov	Dec	Jan	Feb	Mar	Apr	May	Jun	Jul	Aug	Sep	Oct	Nov	Dec

Cox's Orange Pippin
A very popular, traditional variety that produces beautiful, firm-textured, sweet-tasting eating apples – just about as good as an eater can get.

More varieties
- **American Mother:** An old, scab-resistant variety that produces a beautiful, rosy-red, sweet-tasting apple that is good for eating and cooking.
- **Bramley's Seedlings:** One of the best cooking-apple varieties. It produces huge, green-skinned, white-fleshed fruits that are wonderful stewed or in pies.
- **Egremont Russet:** A very good, tried-and-trusted old eating variety that produces a characteristic, matt-skinned, orange-yellow fruit that has a good bite.
- **James Grieve:** A reliable, hardy, early variety that produces a slightly soft-textured fruit – perfect if you prefer an easy bite.

SOIL AND SITE NEEDS

Apples do best in a deep, loamy or brick-earthy soil that is neither very wet and heavy nor dry and sandy. If your soil is overly dry and sandy, clayey or waterlogged, you will have to make adjustments. Prepare the ground by double digging. Break through the hard 'pan' or subsoil. Dig in well-rotted farmyard manure, wood ash, and compost – anything to give the ground a bit of body. Plant the trees on the north and east sides of the plot so that, while they are sheltered by neighbouring trees and plots, they themselves do not cast shadows over your plot. You need to talk to your neighbours.

PLANTING PROCEDURES

- November–March for bare-rooted trees, and any time for container-grown – dig a hole that is 60 cm (2 ft) deep, and 90 cm–1.2 m (3–4 ft) in diameter.
- For a 2–3-year-old, bare-rooted tree – trim broken and torn roots.
- For a container-grown tree – remove the container.
- Set a bare-rooted tree in the hole, so that the topmost roots are 7.5–10 cm (3–4 in) below the surface, and support with a vertical stake.
- Set a container-grown tree in the hole so that the top of its compost is level with the surface, and support with an angled stake that points into the wind.
- Put a small amount of spent manure or compost into the hole and then fill with well-trodden topsoil.

PLANT CARE

Prune as the buds appear in spring, or in autumn if you planted in March. Create a framework of stout branches. Cut the leading shoots back to half the length of the branch. Cut inwardly growing branches right back. With cordons, shorten side or lateral shoots to within 2–3 buds of the stem.

Cut back leading shoots

Choose four good branches

HARVESTING

Pick the apples when they are 'just ripe', when they part readily from the spur. As a test, take the apple and raise it to a horizontal position; if it is ready, it will come away with no more than a very slight twist.

TROUBLESHOOTING

- **Sticky curling leaves** Most likely to be aphids. Shows as curling leaves, distorted shoots, and fruit drop. Avoid the problem by spraying in winter with a winter oil wash to destroy the eggs.
- **Apple scab** Shows itself as green-brown splotches on the leaves and fruits, and eventually as scabby fruits and dropping leaves. Burn damaged fruits and leaves. Avoid the problem by planting resistant varieties.

Blackberries

If you enjoy the notion of picking and eating soft fruits, and there is some room on one of your boundaries, then blackberries are a good option. Just think about it – if every plant provides 5–12 kg (10–25 lb) of fruits, you could be having jam today, and jam tomorrow!

PLANT BARE-ROOTED (Plant container-grown any time)   **HARVEST**

Jan	Feb	Mar	Apr	May	Jun	Jul	Aug	Sep	Oct	Nov	Dec	Jan	Feb	Mar	Apr	May	Jun	Jul	Aug	Sep	Oct	Nov	Dec

Himalaya Giant
A very popular, reliable, vigorous, late-cropping variety that produces heavy crops of large, black, high-acid fruits – perfect for jam-making.

More varieties

- **Bedford Giant:** A well-known, vigorous, early-cropping variety that produces large bunches of sweet-flavoured fruits. The large size makes this a good choice for the allotment.

- **Fantasia:** A relatively new, vigorous, late-cropping variety that produces unusually large fruits.

- **John Innes:** A good, old-fashioned, late-cropping dessert variety. It produces large, sweet fruits.

- **Merton Thornless:** A low-growing, thornless, late-cropping variety that produces large, fat fruits with a good taste. It does not produce a huge crop, but the complete lack of thorns makes cropping an easy task – good where there are children.

SOIL AND SITE NEEDS

Blackberries do well in just about any ordinary soil as long as it is deeply dug, well manured and free from puddled water. They really suffer if their roots are in waterlogged ground. If the ground is light and sandy, spread a thick mulch of well-rotted farmyard manure over it to hold in moisture. Blackberries do best when they are planted in rows that run from north to south. The morning sun shines on the east-facing side of the row, midday sun shines down the length of the row, and the evening sun shines on the west-facing side.

PLANTING PROCEDURES

- March–April and December for bare-rooted canes, and any time for container-grown – dig a trench that is 23 cm (9 in) deep and 60 cm (2 ft) wide.
- Spread about 10 cm (4 in) of well-rotted manure on the bottom of the trench and set the bare-rooted canes in place, spaced 1.8 m (6 ft) apart. Set container-grown plants so that the top of their compost is level with the soil.
- Fill the trench up with well-rotted manure topped with compacted soil.
- Build a 1.8 m (6 ft) high post and wire support fence – with horizontal wires at 30 cm (1 ft) intervals.

PLANT CARE

After planting, cut down the canes to about 23 cm (9 in) above the soil – each cut above a strong, healthy bud. During the summer, weave and train the young canes along all but the top wire. In the second year, train the new canes up through to the top wire. In the autumn, cut down all fruiting canes. Repeat the procedure in all following years.

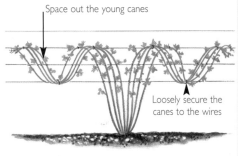

Space out the young canes

Loosely secure the canes to the wires

HARVESTING

Pick the berries when the colour has just changed from red to black, while they are still firm. As a test, take a berry and gently ease it away. If it comes cleanly away from its plug and stalk, then it is ready.

TROUBLESHOOTING

- **Sticky curling leaves** Most likely to be aphids. Shows as leaves that are variously blistered and curled. Large colonies of aphids will result in distorted shoots and fruit drop. Avoid the problem by spraying with a winter oil wash to destroy the eggs. Burn all the cuttings and rubbish at the end of the season.
- **Grey mould** Shows itself as a grey-white, powdery mould. Usually attacks areas where there is a lot of water, or where there are very hot or very cold conditions and little air-flow. Avoid the problem by cutting back the lower foliage, and generally clearing away all the rubbish on the ground.

Currants – black, red and white

I have grouped all the different currants together not because their cultivation is identical – in fact blackcurrants need slightly different treatment from red- and whitecurrants – but more because most people tend to think of them as being very similar.

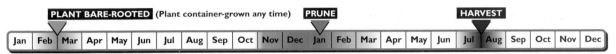

PLANT BARE-ROOTED (Plant container-grown any time)   **PRUNE**   **HARVEST**

| Jan | Feb | Mar | Apr | May | Jun | Jul | Aug | Sep | Oct | Nov | Dec | Jan | Feb | Mar | Apr | May | Jun | Jul | Aug | Sep | Oct | Nov | Dec |

Blanka White Currant
A very popular and vigorous, July-cropping variety that produces heavy crops of big, fat, gold-white berries.

More varieties
- **Baldwin (black):** A very popular, compact, medium-sized, late variety that produces small berries with a characteristic, sweet tart taste. Good for making blackcurrant jam.

- **Boskoop Giant (black):** A large, vigorous, early variety with big, long bunches of large, sweet berries. Good choice for a sheltered, warm corner.

- **Layton's Number 1 (red):** An old, mid-season variety bearing large, prizewinning fruits in big trusses.

- **Red Lake (red):** A vigorous variety that produces long, heavy bunches of good-sized fruits.

- **White Dutch (white):** A reliable variety with big bunches of large, very juicy, sweet-flavoured, golden berries.

SOIL AND SITE NEEDS

Currants can be grown in just about any soil, even if it is rather wet and heavy, but they prefer a light, sandy, well-drained, loamy soil. The ground needs to be deeply worked and well manured before planting. Any hard subsoil should be broken up and worked with plenty of farmyard manure or leafmould. Look for a spot that is moist but well drained. Ideally, the bushes need to be about 1.5 m (5 ft) apart, with plenty of sun, and a good circulation of air, with some protection from wind on the north and east sides. If your allotment is very exposed, you could build screens on the windward side.

PLANTING PROCEDURES

- November or late February–March for bare-rooted bushes, and any time for container-grown – dig a hole that is wide and deep enough for the roots to spread out.
- Spread about 10 cm (4 in) of well-rotted manure over the bottom of the hole and set the bare-rooted bush in place. Set container-grown plants so that the fill is level with the soil.
- Fill the hole up with well-rotted manure topped up with well-compacted soil.

PLANT CARE

After planting blackcurrants, cut all stems down to about 2.5 cm (1 in) above soil level, and in the following season cut out all shoots that have produced fruits. With red- and whitecurrants, cut the main shoots back by half immediately after planting. In late winter, cut out shoots that cross the plant's centre.

Blackcurrant, first season after pruning

Red- or whitecurrant, pruned as a bush

HARVESTING

Pick the fruits immediately the colour has turned, while the berries are still firm and shiny. It is best to pick off the whole cluster rather than individual berries. In a good year, you might need to do this once or twice a week.

TROUBLESHOOTING

- **Vanishing berries** Given the chance, birds will strip the berries. Avoid the problem by growing the bushes in a netted cage.
- **Brown-ringed holes in the leaves** Likely to be the dreaded capsid bug. A heavy attack will result in distorted shoots and fruit drop. Spray with a winter wash. Avoid the problem by growing a resistant variety.

Gooseberries

For the whole of my childhood, in our garden there was a totally neglected gooseberry bush that gave us a good crop of gorgeous golden fruits every year without fail. This demonstrates just how easy it is to grow and enjoy gooseberries.

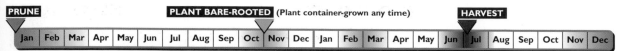

PRUNE								PLANT BARE-ROOTED (Plant container-grown any time)										HARVEST					
Jan	Feb	Mar	Apr	May	Jun	Jul	Aug	Sep	Oct	Nov	Dec	Jan	Feb	Mar	Apr	May	Jun	Jul	Aug	Sep	Oct	Nov	Dec

Leveller

A very popular and reliable, yellow-green, dual eating-cooking variety that produces large, down-covered fruits. If you only have room for a single bush, this is the one to go for.

More varieties

- **Black Velvet:** An award-winning, mildew-resistant variety that produces heavy yields of dark red, grape-sized fruits. A good choice – good colour, good flavour and completely resistant to the feared mildew.

- **Careless:** A very popular, old, grow-anywhere, yellow-green, cooking variety that produces smooth, crisp-textured, medium-sized fruits.

- **Hinnonmaki:** A mildew-resistant variety that produces big, fat, red, superb-tasting gooseberries; very popular in America and Europe.

- **Keepsake:** An extra-early, light green, cooking variety with medium-sized fruits. This is the one to choose if you like gooseberry pies and tarts.

SOIL AND SITE NEEDS

Gooseberries do well in just about any deeply dug, well-manured, medium to heavy loam soil. That said, most varieties are more susceptible to moulds and mildews when they are grown on heavy land than when grown on a light, sandy soil. The soil needs to be moist but well drained, with plenty of well-rotted manure to hold in the moisture. Avoid low-lying, boggy areas. Although gooseberries are hardy and will grow in more or less any position, they do best in a sunny, open, airy spot that is sheltered on the north and east sides.

PLANTING PROCEDURES

- October–November or late February–March for bare-rooted bushes, and at any time for container-grown – dig a hole that is wide and deep enough for the roots to spread out.
- Spread about 10 cm (4 in) of well-rotted manure over the bottom of the hole and set the bare-rooted bush in place. Set container-grown plants so that the top of their compost is level with the soil.
- Fill the hole up with a mixture of topsoil and well-rotted manure, topped with well-compacted soil.

PLANT CARE

After planting, cut back each main branch by about half. In the following autumn, cut back by half all the shoots that have formed during the year. At the end of the following season, shorten those shoots produced during the season by half and clear out any shoots that crowd out the centre.

HARVESTING

Pick fruits for cooking as soon as they start to colour (while still hard), and fruits for eating when they feel slightly soft to the touch. In a good year, you might need to gather the berries once or twice a week.

Shorten the young shoots in the 1st and 2nd seasons, so that you have a well-shaped bush

TROUBLESHOOTING

- **Curling, distorted leaves** Likely to be aphids. Spray with an oil-derived winter wash.
- **Holes in leaves** Probably the very common gooseberry sawfly. In the winter, remove all the soil and litter around the plant to a depth of about 7.5–10 cm (3–4 in) and burn it, and then spray with a winter wash.

Pears

If your aim is to stay with the same allotment plot for five years or more, then planting a bare-rooted maiden pear tree and training it as an espalier is a very good option. If you are lucky, you will have delicious fruits to enjoy within 4–5 years.

										PLANT BARE-ROOTED	(Plant container-grown any time)									HARVEST			PRUNE	
Jan	Feb	Mar	Apr	May	Jun	Jul	Aug	Sep	Oct	Nov	Dec	Jan	Feb	Mar	Apr	May	Jun	Jul	Aug	Sep	Oct	Nov	Dec

Conference
A very popular – perhaps the most popular – self-fertile, dessert variety that produces long, compact fruits. This is the best one to choose if you like your pears firm.

More varieties
- **Beurre Bedford Hardy:** A vigorous, self-fertile variety bearing medium-sized, greenish-yellow, dessert pears.

- **Durondeau:** A partially self-fertile, compact-growing variety that bears medium-sized, yellow to red fruits. It is a good choice for a warm, sheltered allotment.

- **Louise Bonne of Jersey:** A reliable, tried-and-trusted, old, partially self-fertile, dessert variety that produces medium-sized, red-flushed, greenish-yellow fruits that are ready to pick towards the end of September.

- **William's Bon Chretien:** A much-loved, old, self-fertile variety that produces big, fat, musky-flavoured, pink-blushed, yellow-green fruits.

SOIL AND SITE NEEDS

Although pears do best when they are planted in well-drained loam, a pear grown in a well-drained, heavy soil will generally do better than one grown in either a dry, light sand or in a dry, heavy clay. The site is very important: they need a warm, sheltered, frost-free corner, with a windbreak to the exposed north and east sides. If you are concerned about your site, then avoid problems by protecting the pears with temporary nets or plastic screens. Above all, pears dislike cold, wind and waterlogged soil.

PLANTING PROCEDURES

- October–November for a bare-rooted maiden – dig a hole that is 45 cm (18 in) deep and 7.5–15 cm (3–6 in) in diameter. Break up the subsoil, and top with a thin layer of broken brick.
- Set the bare-rooted tree in the hole, so that the topmost roots are 7.5–10 cm (3–4 in) below the surface.
- Fill the hole with loamy topsoil and tread firm.

PLANT CARE

For details on how to grow a tree or bush form, see Apples (page 67). For an espalier, after planting build a small fence-like frame with wires. Prune the bare-rooted maiden down to about 38 cm (15 in). During

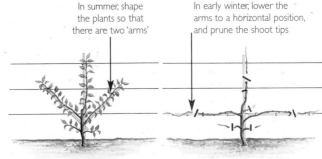

In summer, shape the plants so that there are two 'arms'

In early winter, lower the arms to a horizontal position, and prune the shoot tips

the summer, tie the shoots into the wires. In the early winter, carefully lower the 'arms' into a horizontal position and tie them in place. Prune the tips of each shoot back to a healthy bud. Repeat this procedure in the following years.

HARVESTING

Pick fruits for cooking as soon as they start to colour (while still hard). Take the pear between cupped palms and, being very careful not to damage the skin, gently lever it off. It should come away with no more than a slight twist.

TROUBLESHOOTING

- **Falling fruits** Almost certainly the common pear midge. The midges lay eggs in the blossom, and these become maggots within the pears. The affected pears deform and drop to the ground. Control the problem by routinely picking up fruits and leaves, and by deep-hoeing the soil.

Plums

Some people may have visions of 6 m (20 ft) high plum trees that you will need to climb in order to pick the fruits, but if you opt to grow a bush type, or a half-standard, you could be eating delicious plums without any need for such acrobatics.

(Plant container-grown any time) **PLANT BARE-ROOTED**　　(For training) **PRUNE**　　　**PRUNE**　　**HARVEST**

Jan	Feb	Mar	Apr	May	Jun	Jul	Aug	Sep	Oct	Nov	Dec	Jan	Feb	Mar	Apr	May	Jun	Jul	Aug	Sep	Oct	Nov	Dec

Purple Pershore

A disease-resistant, heavy-cropping variety with medium-sized, blue-purple, purple-fleshed fruits that are really good for stewed plums and jam-making.

More varieties

- **Denniston's Superb:** A tried-and-trusted, reliable, hardy variety that produces large, pink-blushed, greenish-yellow, very juicy fruits.

- **Early Laxton:** A very popular, early-fruiting, partially self-fertile variety with small, yellowish, pink-blushed, golden-fleshed fruits that are good for eating in the hand.

- **Giant Prune:** A heavy-cropping, self-fertile, disease- and frost-resistant, cooking variety bearing large, dark red, purple-fleshed fruits.

- **Victoria:** A reliable, dual eating-cooking, self-fertile variety that bears large crops of fat, juicy, red-gold fruits – perfect for eating in the hand, and for serving with apples and custard.

SOIL AND SITE NEEDS

The plum will do fine in just about any loamy soil, as long as the subsoil is well drained. If the soil is too damp, the tree will show a lot of foliage and not much fruit. The ideal is a warm, loamy soil that is light rather than heavy. As for the site, the ideal is an open plot that slopes to the southwest, so there is plenty of sunshine, a free circulation of air, and good shelter to the north and the east. Plums do not thrive in deep shade.

PLANTING PROCEDURES

- October–November for a bare-rooted, two-year old bush – dig a hole that is 60 cm (2 ft) deep and 7.5–15 cm (3–6 in) in diameter. Break up the subsoil and top it with a thin layer of broken brick.
- Set the bare-rooted tree in the hole, so that the topmost roots are no more than 7.5–10 cm (3–4 in) below the surface, and support it with a stake.
- Fill the hole with loamy topsoil and tread firm.

PLANT CARE

For trees and espaliers, refer to the advice given for both apples and pears (pages 67 and 71). For a bush, wait until spring and cut the central stem down to 7.5–15 cm (3–6 in) high. During the following spring, cut back half of the new growth to just beyond an outward-facing bud. Cut out at their bases all secondary shoots. In subsequent summers, thin out crossing branches and remove suckers.

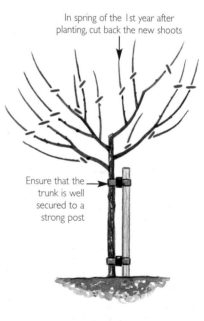

In spring of the 1st year after planting, cut back the new shoots

Ensure that the trunk is well secured to a strong post

HARVESTING

Gather the plums as soon as the colour changes, while they still feel firm to the touch. If you are unsure, hold back until the flavour develops. If you pick too soon, the flavour will fail. Pick the plums separately – never in clusters.

TROUBLESHOOTING

- **Falling fruits** Probably the common plum sawfly. The grubs of this insect eat into the young fruits causing them to fall. Control the problem by routinely picking up and burning fruits and leaves, by deep-hoeing the soil, and by spraying with a winter wash.
- **Curling-leaf aphids** Shows as curled edges to the leaves, fruit fall, and general weakening of the tree. Spray the tree with a winter wash and burn all rubbish.

Raspberries

Raspberries and their close relations, the raspberry-blackberry hybrids such as loganberries, veitchberries, lowberries and one or two others, are always a good option for the allotment. Choose a variety that suits your particular location.

(Plant container-grown any time) **PLANT BARE-ROOTED** **PRUNE** **HARVEST** **PRUNE**

Jan	Feb	Mar	Apr	May	Jun	Jul	Aug	Sep	Oct	Nov	Dec	Jan	Feb	Mar	Apr	May	Jun	Jul	Aug	Sep	Oct	Nov	Dec

Malling Orion

An old, early, vigorous, heavy-cropping, summer-fruiting variety that produces medium-sized pinkish fruits with a good texture and taste.

More varieties

- **Glen Clova:** A very reliable and popular, heavy-cropping, summer-fruiting variety that produces medium–small, red berries. The berries can be a bit on the small side, but their taste and texture are good.

- **Malling Admiral:** A strong-growing, disease-resistant, summer-fruiting variety that produces large, fat, firm-textured, bright red berries.

- **Malling Promise:** A heavy-cropping, summer-fruiting, disease-resistant variety that produces large, red-orange fruits. The taste is a bit flat, but it does well in most soils.

- **Zeva:** A hardy, medium-sized, autumn-fruiting variety with large, red fruits. It does well on difficult, windy plots.

SOIL AND SITE NEEDS

Summer-fruiting raspberries do well in a well-drained, light soil, as long as the soil is given a good mulch of rotted manure in times of drought. That said, they can be planted in a heavier, clay soil, as long the ground is free from standing water. They like a sheltered, sunny position, away from draughts and deep shade. Ideally, the rows should run north to south so that the canes receive maximum sun. Autumn-fruiting raspberries require much the same conditions – full sun and a light soil – but they need a spot that is extra sheltered, yet at the same time well ventilated.

PLANTING PROCEDURES

- November–December for bare-rooted canes – double dig the ground with plenty of well-rotted manure, and dig a trench 15 cm (6 in) deep and 45 cm (18 in) wide.
- Set the bare-rooted canes in the trench at about 45 cm (18 in) apart in rows 1.5–1.8 m (5–6 ft) apart.
- Fill the trench with a mixture of topsoil and old manure, and tread firm.

PLANT CARE

Build a support frame with horizontal wires at 60 cm (2 ft), 90 cm (3 ft) and 1.5 m (5 ft) from the ground. After planting, cut all the canes down to 23–30 cm (9–12 in) high. When new canes start to grow, cut the old 23–30 cm (9–12 in) high canes down to soil level. Tie the new growing canes to the support wires. After fruiting, cut all fruiting canes down to soil level, and tie up all the new canes.

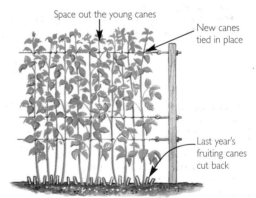

Space out the young canes

New canes tied in place

Last year's fruiting canes cut back

HARVESTING

Raspberries should be picked on a dry, sunny day, as soon as they are fully coloured. You can snip them off complete with the stalk, or pull the fruits clear of the stalks. This is also a good time to remove and burn damaged, maggoty berries before the various pests can escape.

TROUBLESHOOTING

- **Curling-leaf aphids** Shows as curled edges to the leaves, premature fruit fall, and general weakening of the canes. Spray the canes with a winter wash and burn all the rubbish.
- **Maggoty fruits** Most likely to be caused by the raspberry beetle. The beetles feed on the flowers and lay eggs that eventually produce grubs that attack the berries. Avoid the problem by burning old canes as soon as they are cut, by generally clearing up rubbish, and by spraying with a winter wash in December.

Rhubarb

Rhubarb has a very distinctive taste that people either love or hate. The good news is that most children love it, especially when it is buried under custard or made into a rhubarb crumble. The plants will do very well in a corner that is not too dry, shady or wet.

PLANT ROOT **HARVEST**

Jan	Feb	Mar	Apr	May	Jun	Jul	Aug	Sep	Oct	Nov	Dec	Jan	Feb	Mar	Apr	May	Jun	Jul	Aug	Sep	Oct	Nov	Dec

Victoria
A tried-and-trusted variety. An old catalogue, dating from about 1910, describes this as being 'late but well worth the waiting'.

More varieties
- **Glaskins Perpetual** A reliable, long-cropping, easy-grow variety that produces bright red, full-flavoured stems over a long period.
- **Green Victoria** A tender, green, upright, heavy-cropping variety that produces big, thick, upright, green stalks. It has a tart flavour.
- **Hawkes Champagne:** A reliable, old, early variety with thick, rosy-red stalks that are perfect for crumbles and pies. Good for forcing.
- **Macdonald's Crimson:** A vigorous Canadian variety that produces large, red to pink stalks, with a tender skin, good-length stalks, and a strong flavour. It is very popular in Canada – you might have to grow it from seed.

SOIL AND SITE NEEDS

The ideal soil is a deep, rich loam that is cool, moist and well drained. Rhubarb does not like boggy, waterlogged soil. In preparation, the soil should be double dug in the autumn, and enriched with plenty of manure. The ideal site for early varieties is warm and well drained, with protection from cold north and east winds, with the ground sloping to the southwest. Later varieties can stand a more open position and a heavier soil. Rhubarb needs plenty of moisture all through the growing season so, although a low, wet situation is unsuitable, a very dry soil is equally useless.

PLANTING PROCEDURES

- February–March for divided roots – in ground that has been previously double dug with plenty of rank manure, dig a 30 cm (1 ft) deep hole that is wide enough to take the spread of the roots.
- Set the plants 75 cm (30 in) apart, in rows 90 cm (3 ft) apart.
- Fill around the root with a mixture of topsoil and old manure, and tread firm.

Protect from frost with straw when shoots appear

Cover to force plant to grow

75 cm (30 in)

90 cm (3 ft)

Moisture-retentive soil

Harvest by pulling off a complete stick; do not use the leaves

PLANT CARE

As soon as the planting is complete, stir the surface of the soil to prevent caking, and cover the ground with a mulch of well-rotted manure. Water as often as possible. Remove flower stems as soon as they appear, as these 'exhaust' the plant. Force the crop by covering the plants with straw and black plastic sheeting.

HARVESTING

Gather the stalks from mid-February to mid-July. To pull, hold the stalk firmly and give it a half-turn tug so that it shears away from the crown. Trim the leaves off with a knife and put them on the compost heap.

TROUBLESHOOTING

- **Crown rot** Shows itself as soft, brown areas to the side of the crown, with the stalks and shoots looking weak and spindly. Takes about two years to get a hold, and is not much of a problem in the first year, but can totally wipe out the crop from then onwards. Burn the affected plant and grow a new variety in a different part of the allotment.

Strawberries

There is simply no comparison between delicious home-grown strawberries and the ones that you find on sale in the supermarkets. An allotment strawberry might not be nearly as big, but its colour, texture and flavour will both surprise and delight you.

Jan	Feb	Mar	Apr	May	Jun	Jul	Aug	Sep	Oct	Nov	Dec	Jan	Feb	Mar	Apr	May	Jun	Jul	Aug	Sep	Oct	Nov	Dec

PLANT BARE-ROOTED (Plant container-grown any time)   **HARVEST**   **PRUNE**

Cambridge Favourite

A heavy-cropping, virus- and disease-resistant, early variety with medium-sized, orange-red fruits that are not as plump or as juicy as some, but this is still one of the most popular varieties.

More varieties

- **Cambridge Vigour:** A tried-and-trusted, very popular, summer-fruiting variety that produces big, fat, pear-shaped fruits with lots of flavour.

- **Honeoye:** A heavy-cropping, early summer-fruiting variety that produces dark red, slightly soft fruits.

- **Pegasus:** A disease-resistant, mid-season variety. The berries are a good size, and the flavour is fine, but the texture tends towards being soft.

- **Tantallon:** A heavy-cropping, disease-resistant, summer-fruiting variety that produces small to medium-sized fruits. This is a good variety to grow if you are having trouble with various blights and mildews.

SOIL AND SITE NEEDS

While strawberries do best on a deep, heavy loam that is inclined to clay, they can be grown on just about any well-cultivated soil – even if it is a bit sandy and stony – as long as the soil is kept moist in the dry summer months. If the soil is overly wet, sour, cold, overshadowed by trees or subject to cold draughts, the crop will be disappointing. The ideal aspect is a site that slopes down to the south or southeast, with protection on the north and northeast sides. In preparation, the soil needs to be deeply dug with lots of farmyard manure.

PLANTING PROCEDURES

- Double dig the ground incorporating plenty of well-rotted manure.
- July–September for bare-rooted plants – dig shallow holes that are wide enough to take the roots at full spread, in rows 60 cm (2 ft) apart, with the plants 45 cm (18 in) apart in the rows.
- 'Puddle' the plants in place, carefully spread the roots out to their full extent, top up with friable soil, ease and lift the plant slightly, and press the soil firm.

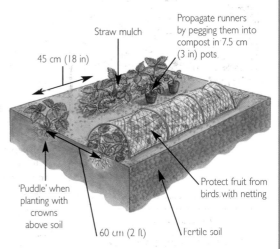

Straw mulch

Propagate runners by pegging them into compost in 7.5 cm (3 in) pots

45 cm (18 in)

'Puddle' when planting with crowns above soil

60 cm (2 ft)

Protect fruit from birds with netting

Fertile soil

PLANT CARE

When the berries are beginning to form, spread a thick mulch of clean, closely packed straw around the plants to keep them warm and clean, and to hold back the weeds. Push in sticks or wires to make a low, bow-shaped support, and spread a net to keep the birds off.

HARVESTING

Pick the strawberries as they ripen, as soon as the colour is uniform. The best time is in the early morning when the berries are dry. Pick the berries complete with the stalks and plugs.

TROUBLESHOOTING

- **Slugs** Bites and holes appear in the berries. Gather the slugs and snails by hand.
- **Shrivelled fruits** Probably a mould or mildew. Avoid the problem by growing a disease-resistant variety in a well-ventilated, sunny spot.
- **Blackened flowers** Probably frost damage. Avoid the problem by covering the strawberries with a fine fleece.

Growing herbs

Are herbs suitable for the allotment?

Culinary herbs are a natural component of an allotment, and they are perfect for planting in and around the vegetables, salads and other crops. I can think of nothing better than to spend a day working at the allotment and then, when you are tired but beautifully relaxed, harvesting all the makings for a delicious meal, complete with a handful of just-picked herbs, and wending your way home to cook and eat them fresh from the plot.

GETTING STARTED

When thinking about planting culinary herbs, it is best to start with the most common plants – mint, parsley, chives, sage – and then try the more unusual items when time and space allow. As for the shape of the planting (whether you are going to plant them randomly, in formal borders or in pots), a good method is to start by planting herbs in odd corners, so that you can get to grips with their soil and site needs; then, when you know them better, you can be a bit more ambitious.

MEDICINAL HERBS

Whereas culinary herbs are used in cooking because they smell good, taste good, look good and to some extent do us good, medicinal herbs are grown specifically for their healing properties, and are not covered in this book.

If you are considering planting and using medicinal herbs, you must seek and follow specialist advice.

HERB GARDENS

A seemingly random medley of herbs and other plants looks just right on an allotment.

Formal, circular, 'cartwheel' designs with colour-contrasting herbs are exciting.

Rustic poles held in place by stakes can create a dedicated area for potted herbs.

Growing them in containers is a good way of controlling the more invasive herbs.

Bay
A hardy, evergreen shrub with dark green, aromatic leaves. In ideal conditions, it can grow to a height of 1.8–3.6 m (6–12 ft). It likes a well-drained, moisture-retentive soil in a sunny position. The leaves give a rich flavour to stews and fish dishes.

Borage
A hardy annual with oval, slightly hairy, green leaves. It grows to a height of about 7.5–15 cm (3–6 in). It can survive in just about any soil, but does best in a well-drained, moisture-retentive soil in full sun. The leaves can be added to cold drinks and used in salads.

Chervil
A hardy biennial that is usually grown as an annual, with bright green, fern-like leaves. It looks a bit like parsley, and grows to a height of about 45 cm (18 in). Chervil prefers a rich, moderately moist soil. The leaves, with their delicate, aniseed flavour, are good in salads and sandwiches, and in fish and egg dishes.

Chives

A hardy, low-growing, clump-forming perennial, with green, tubular stems topped with round, rose-pink flower-heads. It does best in a rich soil in a sheltered, sunny corner, and needs regular watering. The chopped-up stems or leaves have a beautifully distinctive, tart, onion-like flavour.

Dill

A hardy annual with tall stems topped with feathery, blue-green leaves, growing to a height of about 60–90 cm (2–3 ft). It thrives in a well-drained, moderately fertile soil in a sheltered, sunny position. The freshly picked leaves can be used to best effect to garnish and flavour new potatoes and white fish.

Fennel

A hardy herbaceous perennial with tall stems, feathery, green leaves, and golden-yellow flowerheads, growing to about 1.5–1.8 m (5–6 ft). It does best in a moist, well-drained, moderately fertile soil in a sheltered, sunny position. The leaves are good with fish and stews, and the seeds are good in cakes and bread.

Ginger

Tropical perennial that can be grown in containers in temperate climates if the roots are protected in a greenhouse from autumn to late spring, or if it is kept in a heated greenhouse all year. The easiest way to grow ginger in a cool climate, however, is to buy fresh roots in spring, put them in pots and harvest the complete crop in autumn.

Mint

Common mint is a hardy herbaceous perennial with mid-green leaves that grows to about 60 cm (2 ft). It does best in a moisture-retentive, fertile soil in a warm, sheltered position, but seems to grow just about anywhere, and can be invasive. The leaves are perfect when chopped with brown sugar and used with vinegar in the form of a mint sauce.

Parsley

A hardy biennial that tends to be grown as an annual, with curly, tight-packed, green leaves. It does best in moisture-retentive, fertile soil in full sun or shade. The leaves are commonly used in sauces and as a garnish.

Rosemary

An evergreen shrub with narrow, spiky, mid- to dark green, aromatic leaves that grows just about anywhere. The leaves are used to flavour all manner of fish and meat dishes.

Sage

A hardy, evergreen shrub with long, aromatic, green-grey leaves. It does best in fertile soil in a warm, sheltered spot. The leaves are used in a whole range of dishes – everything from sage and onion stuffing to cheese-sage dip.

Thyme

A hardy, dwarf, evergreen shrub with small, aromatic leaves. It grows best in a light, well-drained soil in an airy, sunny position. The leaves are used with fish and rich meats such as hare and pork.

Glossary

Bare-rooted Describes a deciduous shrub or tree that has been lifted from open ground in such a way that there is very little soil around its roots.

Biennial Plant that completes its life cycle over two seasons.

Blanching Technique of whitening a plant by excluding sunlight; for example, blanching green celery or endive to make it white. The act of blanching changes taste and texture for the better.

Brown-site allotment Allotment site situated on reclaimed ground, such as the site of an old factory. Such ground might be difficult to work, with lots of concrete and rubbish, and perhaps also polluted.

Catch crop Fast-growing crop that is grown on ground that is temporarily vacant. The catch crop is sown the moment the main crop has been harvested, and is itself harvested before the next main crop is sown.

Chitting The act of germinating seed prior to sowing, as with potatoes.

Cloche Just about any glass-, plastic-, net- or fleece-covered frame, tent or tunnel used to protect seeds or plants. The term is becoming more and more difficult to define, in that some modern materials such as fine fleece are almost a crossover between plastic sheeting and netting.

Compost Rotted organic material used with or instead of manure.

Crown The part of a plant that is just about at ground level, such as the crown of a carrot or the crown of rhubarb.

Dibber Also called 'dibble' and 'dibby'. Stick, spick or finger-like tool used for making holes in readiness for planting large seeds, seedlings or small plants.

Dressed seed Seed that has been powdered, soaked or otherwise covered in a protective coating that guards against fungus, birds, mice and other problems.

Drill Term used to describe the shallow hole, furrow, V-section trench or U-section trench into which seeds are sown. Also used to describe a line of seeds. Some older gardeners say things such as 'It's time to drill my seeds' or ' That's a good drill bed'.

Earthing up The act of using a rake, hoe, spade or other tool to drag earth up around the base or stem of a plant.

Fertilizer Organic or chemical material used as a plant food.

Forcing Technique of speeding up growth by excluding daylight and boosting warmth; for example, putting an upturned box stuffed with straw over rhubarb.

Friable Positive term used to describe soil when it is slightly moist and fine.

Greens General term used to describe all the green-leaf vegetables such as spinach beet, broccoli, sprouts, cabbage, cauliflower, colewort, kale and others.

Half-hardy Describes a plant that is unable to withstand all but a very mild frost, so cannot survive the winter without protection.

Hardy Describes a plant that can survive the winter without any need for protection.

Holder In the context of an allotment, term used to describe the person who rents the allotment holding. The moment you rent an allotment, or an allotment holding, you are legally termed 'the holder'.

Humus Decomposed organic matter in the soil.

Manure Material of animal origin used to improve the fertility and structure of the soil, such as horse manure, chicken manure or rabbit manure. Because some manures are polluted by pesticides or animal medicines, some organic growers avoid manure in favour of compost.

Mulch Layer of natural material such as compost or crushed bark, or a sheet of material such as plastic, that is spread over the soil so as to hold back weeds and keep in moisture.

Organic allotment One that is managed without the use of chemical fertilizers or sprays; an allotment that is environmentally friendly and people-friendly. To be truly organic, you have to look at every aspect of growing, from preparing the soil and choosing the seeds through to weed control and harvesting the crop. For example, a piece of old foam-backed carpet is a good way of holding back the weeds, but not so good when the foam breaks down and leaches chemicals into the soil. Horse manure is good, but might come from sick horses that have been treated with antibiotics. In the context of an allotment, the best method is to develop your own 'eco-green' or organic way of thinking and then do your best to follow it.

Pan Hard layer between the topsoil and the subsoil.

Patio In an allotment, usually a rough paved area around the shed.

Plot Term used to describe a single allotment holding: an area that measures approximately 10 rods, or 253 square metres (302 square yards) – an area that, according to various Acts of Parliament, is big enough to feed a family of four.

Potting on The act of transferring seedlings into bigger and bigger pots in readiness for their final planting out.

Pricking out Term used to describe the act of using your fingers and a small stick-like tool to transfer small seedlings from a plant box to a pot.

Site The sum total of all the plots; for example, there might be 300 individual plots or holdings on one site.

Spit The depth of a spade; usually about 25 cm (10 in).

Standpipe Water pipe complete with tap, or a pipe connected to a trough.

Stand trough See Standpipe.

Tilth The surface of the soil; the layer that is cultivated.

Index

Acknowledgments

Photographs: **AG&G Books** and **King's Seeds**, Monks Farm, Coggeshall Road,
Kelvedon, Colchester, Essex CO5 9PG, Tel: 01376 570000, www.kingsseeds.com.